By Owen Lattimore

The Desert Road to Turkestan

High Tartary

Manchuria, Cradle of Conflict

The Mongols of Manchuria

Inner Asian Frontiers of China

Mongol Journeys

America and Asia

China, A Short History
(*with Eleanor Lattimore*)

Solution in Asia

The Situation in Asia

The Situation in Asia

OWEN LATTIMORE

The Situation in Asia

An Atlantic Monthly Press Book

Little, Brown and Company · Boston

1949

Published April 1949

1

Published simultaneously
in Canada by McClelland and Stewart Limited

PRINTED IN THE UNITED STATES OF AMERICA
BY THE HADDON CRAFTSMEN, INC., SCRANTON, PA.

FOREWORD

A PART of the historical material in this book was read as a paper delivered to the American Historical Society at its meeting of December 1948 at Washington, D.C., and published in the *Atlantic Monthly* for March 1949. Another part was published in the *Atlantic* for April 1949. Still other passages were first published in the syndicated articles which I have for several years written for Overseas News Agency. They hold the copyright on these articles, and I am grateful to them for their permission to republish. I also wish to acknowledge permission from *Foreign Affairs* for the use of quotations from "Stalin on Revolution" by "Historicus."

My wife worked so hard in helping to get the book ready for the press that in large measure — like all my books — it has become hers.

O. L.

CONTENTS

The Situation in Asia

CHAPTER I

THE RUINS OF EMPIRE

ASIA is out of control. From Suez to the western Pacific we face one problem after another, in one country after another, which we cannot settle either by an American decision or by joint action with countries that we consider our allies.

From the Arab countries to China, the old forms of ascendancy, protectorate, or rule cannot be reasserted by military action. We have already had enough experience to prove that the more modern and highly equipped is the military force that is used, the more expensive is the failure eventually inflicted on it by cheap methods of guerrilla warfare that require no industrial support. An attempt to stun the peoples of Asia by atomic warfare is out of the question, except for madmen. Asia has no highly developed nerve centers to be paralyzed. Atomic warfare — the ultimate in the use of technology for the purpose of conquest — would in Asia only create a poisonous devastation which it would be beyond the resources even of America to revive economically or administer.

Nor can Asia be starved out or coerced economically. Everywhere in Asia the local resources are ample enough to enable the people to survive without being more miserable even if they resist military coercion: and that degree of misery is one which they are prepared to endure. Being willing to hold out, they have the upper hand over us; for we need the oil, rubber, tin, and other products of Asia even more than the peoples of Asia need our capital, tractors, textile and mining machinery, technicians, and teachers.

Asia, to sum it up, has become a part of the world where the great powers can no longer lay down the law as they did in the nineteenth century and the early part of the twentieth century. We must negotiate; and we can only negotiate successfully if people in Asia are as well satisfied with what they get out of negotiated agreements as we are with what we get out of them. This limitation applies to Russia as well as to the other great powers.

The Near East used to be comfortably managed by a system of British alliances with Arab monarchs and chiefs. Today, that fabric of alliances has been ripped across by the rise of Israel. The fact that Israel is so tiny, and yet has been able to throw the Arab world into such disorder, is a warning that new kinds of power are coming into play that cannot be measured by old standards.

Iran and Afghanistan are countries that cannot, in the long run, be held either by troops sent from America or Britain or by American and British air bases. Nor can the political structure of either Iran or Afghanistan be patched up and stabilized by political support or economic aid from Britain and America. Slowly as yet, but with an unmistakable acceleration, the societies of Iran and Afghanistan, like the Arab societies, are moving into a phase of change. In less than ten years the process of social change in these countries will produce economic developments and new political structures unrecognizable in comparison with what now exists.

India and Pakistan have replaced the old Indian Empire. Their relations with each other, with Britain, and with Russia have not yet been stabilized; but one thing is already clear. In 1939, when Britain declared war on Germany, the Indian Empire was not consulted. By Britain's declaration, it was automatically at war; and all through the war the allocation of Indian resources to the war effort and of Indian manpower to various battlefields was determined not in India by Indians, but in London by the British. It is a truth not usually emphasized, but nevertheless the truth, that Britain could not have survived, and could not have held North Africa and the Near East, without the men and resources drawn from India. But in a third world war, if there is to be one, these decisions will not be made in Britain. India and Pakistan will be at war only if they make their own decisions in New Delhi and Karachi, and only if they decide on war in their own interests.

In Burma, politics is a deadly serious business. Parties are armed, and carry their disagreements into battle; but the amazing development, which no one could have predicted while either the British or the

Japanese held Burma, is that all principal parties, even though they fight each other, are avowedly Marxist.

In colonial Asia, Indonesia, Malaya, and Indo-China all used to be great revenue producers for Western Europe. What they produced, moreover, was of international strategic significance like rubber, tin, oil, bauxite, kapok, and quinine. Political manifestations were weak in all three countries. They could be held in check by a minimum show of force. Today, all three countries are a drain on the countries trying to retain or reassert control over them, though Malaya may still be showing the British some profit on balance. Malaya is held by the Brigade of Guards, the elite troops of the British Army. The Dutch have an estimated 125,000 men in Indonesia, and the French over 100,000 in Indo-China.

China was once a country in which foreign investments were safer than the investments of powerful Chinese. Today, after twenty years of civil war, foreign invasion, and renewed civil war, China is beyond control. Whether Russia can eventually assert control is a question to be considered later; but three years of effort by American political, economic, and military advisors, and two billion dollars of American expenditures between August 1945 and the end of 1948, failed completely to produce a government to the liking of America.

In an Asia out of control, the situation in Japan looks at first glance like the one exception. But in Japan, too, the future is uncertain. The American policy of making Japan both a workshop for Asia and a bulwark against Russia is based on assumptions that within a year will begin to seem much less valid than they did in 1948. Japan is a workshop without raw materials, and a bulwark manned by defenders who may in their own good time decide to deal with the other side. Economically, America does not have a surplus of raw materials big enough to take the place of everything that Japan used to draw from Asia. Politically and militarily, America is not being kept in Japan by a Japanese demand for protection against Russia. The ruling consideration is the American demand for a position of advantage against Russia. The fact that the situation has these two aspects means that Japan is not under unchallengeable control. On the contrary, the chances are increasingly in favor of Japan's ability to play America's need against whatever Russia — and China — may have to offer.

Since the defeat of Germany and Japan the vistas of a new era of world politics have been opening out before us more swiftly than the traditional policies of the great powers could be adjusted to deal with new conditions and problems. In the change from old and familiar standards of power and politics, Asia is linked with Europe. We are rapidly being forced to realize that there is not a single major problem in Europe that can be worked out satisfactorily unless Asia is taken into the calculation.

What we face is nothing less than the necessity to abandon a large part of the patched-together thinking that has passed for statesmanship since the end of the war. The first delusion to be abandoned is the assumption that we can deal with the world's problems in one-two-three order: first Russia; then Europe, as the key position from which to halt the spread of Russian power and influence; then Asia, to the extent that it is important for Europe's economic recovery. All of these problems are interdependent. All must therefore be dealt with simultaneously, with due regard to their interaction on each other. It was so determined for us by what happened during the war, as well as by our policy aims since the war.

During the war, while Germany occupied France and contained Britain, Japan was able to destroy the old structure of empire in Asia beyond the possibility of restoration. Then the Allied victory destroyed both Japan's empire in Asia and Germany's empire in Eastern Europe and the Balkans. The surge of victory, however, was not strong enough to carry Britain, France, and Holland back to full control of their old empires. Their inability to reoccupy and rebuild the ruins of empire left the way open for three new manifestations: the spread of American power and influence; the spread of Russian power and influence; and the rise of new forms of power in Asia.

The fact that both Russia and America have greatly widened their orbits of control and influence has been recognized by everyone. The importance of the third manifestation — the rise in Asia of new forms of power not subject to the old forms of imperial control — has been seriously underestimated. Yet the Asia which succumbed to cheap and rapid conquest in the eighteenth and nineteenth centuries has shown a formidable ability to resist modern armies equipped with planes, tanks, motorized transport, and mobile artillery. The old arithmetic of Asia was a temptation to strong countries. Small forces conquered large territories. The returns, first in loot, then in direct taxation, and finally in trade, investment, and long-term exploitation, paid off the capital cost with incredible rapidity. The new arithmetic is discouraging. The most determined attempts to restore imperial control are those that have been made in Malaya, Indonesia, and Indo-China. The results, except, perhaps, in Malaya, where there is no united nationalist movement, indicate that even if, eventually, the countries can be conquered and "pacified," the capital cost will be so heavy that in order to recover the investment a longer period of peaceful trade, political submissiveness, and docile labor conditions will be needed than any sound banker would be willing to predict. The results of the British, Dutch, and French attempts at direct reconquest check closely with the results of the American attempt in China to maintain indirect control by backing one side against the other in a civil war.

The ability of Asia to resist control radiates an influence on world politics in three directions simultaneously: toward Western Europe, toward America, and toward Russia. Europe's political power in Asia has decreased, but Europe's economic dependence on Asia is as great as it ever was. Either Europe must live indefinitely on a dole from America, or it must recover some at least of its old channels of interchange with Asia: Europe needs raw materials from Asia, and can sell to Asia both consumer goods and capital goods for industrial development. Every failure to reopen these old channels by the use of military force increases the pressure on Europe to resort to negotiation, on terms that will win the consent of Asia.

The countries that are affected by this pressure are key countries. The Western Union countries of Europe, which have been selected by American policy as the nucleus of an Atlantic Pact, are Britain, France, Belgium, Holland, and Luxembourg. Of these, only Luxembourg has no colonies. Belgium has vast holdings in Africa, Holland in Asia. Britain and France have colonial possessions in both Africa and Asia, and in Asia they have important investments and trade interests outside of their own possessions. From the point of view of the American interest, any European country that is fighting in Asia instead of trading with Asia has a hole in its pocket. Marshall Plan money put in the pockets of Britain, France, or Holland is not a good risk if it is going to run out through the hole of chronic warfare against colonial guerrillas, or of uneconomically high expenditure on the policing of countries that are only nominally pacified.

The relationship of Asia to Russia is of a different kind. Russia is the only great power whose home population is in direct contact with Asia along a land frontier. America is separated from Asia by wide oceans. So is Europe, for all practical purposes. Though Europe is a peninsula projecting from the Eurasian land mass, the Western European nations have always moved by water, not by land, in making their conquests in Asia and in trading with Asia. Only a few Americans and Europeans go to Asia. Only rich people in Asia can travel to Europe and America. Ordinary people have only a hazy idea of what European countries and the United States are like, as countries. In Turkey, Iran, Afghanistan, China, Mongolia, and Korea, on the other hand, there are millions of people who are conscious of the Russians not as just another country, but as permanent neighbors. For such people, Russia is not a fabulous country. No propaganda can hide from them the fact that there is both good and bad in Russia. No Russian propaganda can prevent some people among Russia's neighbors from fearing her; no propaganda against Russia can prevent others from envying some of the things that Russia has. Things that Russia's neighbors fear are discussed in later chapters. The things that are admired or envied are where the competition lies — for example, the schools, universities, hospitals, industrial developments, modernized farming, and opportunities for skilled workers that Russia has in greater abundance than any of its neighbors in Asia.

For such reasons as these, the psychological relationship between Asia and Russia is quite different from the relationship between America and Russia. It is practically impossible to persuade the ordinary American worker or farmer that conditions in Russia will ever be as good as they are in America. All that he knows about Russia is words. If the words come from a pro-Russian American, he is suspicious; if they come from Russia's own propaganda, he is even more sus-

picious. Among those peoples in Asia who live near
the Russian frontier, on the other hand, it is impossible
to hide the fact that Russia has progressed much farther
than their own countries. What these people say about
Russia is passed on by word of mouth to others who
live farther from the frontier. The propaganda that
counts in Asia therefore is not Russia's own propaganda but the competing propaganda, among those
who live near Russia, between those who have something bad to say and those who have something good
to say.

While one line of American interest runs through
Europe to Asia, another line runs through Asia to
Russia. The spread of Russian influence into Asia is
upsetting to Europe and America. The spread of direct Russian control over Asia would be disastrous for
the countries of Asia as well as for America and
Europe. To replace one kind of empire with another
kind of empire would make things worse, not better.
For Russia the problem of Asia is much vaster and
more complex than the problem of Eastern Europe,
and the Russians may not be able to assert control in
the same manner. As an alternative they may have to
work out relations with Asia that will be acceptable to
the peoples of Asia and this is a possibility that Western statesmen cannot afford to overlook.

It is this question of the kind of relations acceptable
to Asia that is crucial. Linked with it is the question
of the degree to which countries in Asia may themselves take the initiative in setting the standards of
relationship which are workable because they are

mutually acceptable. The part played by Asia in regrouping the complex of international relations between Asia, Europe, America, and Russia may prove to be more decisive than the parts played even by America and Russia.

There will of course be competition between America and Russia to exercise influence in Asia. There will always be a tendency for American policy to support vested European interests in Asia against the spread of new Russian interests. America's own interests in Asia, however, are not identical with those of Europe, so that there will also be competition in Asia between American and European interests. Because of this diversity of the competing interests, the countries of Asia have an increasing freedom of maneuver.

In order to analyze the potentials of maneuver, the recent history of Asia must be reviewed. Asia is out of control, but not all of Asia is equally out of control. Nor are nationalist revolution, internal social revolution, and economic change at equal levels of development all through Asia. In studying politics amid the ruins of empire, we must take, as a starting point, the great age of empire.

CHAPTER II

HERITAGE OF EMPIRE

THE great age of empire was the second half of the nineteenth century. It opened with a hardening of the lines of power politics in the reaction that followed the European revolutions of 1848. Then came fifty years marked by Perry's opening of Japan, the Crimean War, the Indian Mutiny, Russia's acquisition of the Amur and Ussuri territories, and the Taiping and Moslem rebellions in China. The American Civil War and the emancipation of the serfs in Russia were followed by the filling up of the American West and by vast Russian conquests in Turkistan. The fifty years wound up with the Sino-Japanese War of 1894–1895, the Spanish-American War, the completion of the Trans-Siberian and Chinese Eastern Railways, the enunciation of the Open Door Doctrine, and the Boxer Rebellion in China.

In the heart of this period the British and French took the lead in building up the Treaty Port system in China which was the structural framework of the "Unequal Treaties" curtailing China's sovereignty and giving foreigners a position of privilege. The process actually began with the British-imposed Treaty of

Nanking, accepted in 1842 and ratified in 1843, at the close of the Opium War. As early as 1844 the American policy in China was defined in the Treaty of Wanghia: it was to be a policy refraining from territorial concessions, but emphasizing most-favored-nation status, or "me too" equality in enjoying any rights or privileges conceded by China to any foreign nation.

In this great age of empire there was an unceasing redistribution of power among the great nations which, standing outside of Asia, projected their control into Asia. The shares of power passed from hand to hand; but any hand that held a share of this kind of power could be stretched out over Asia. Three types of empire marked the period.

The British Empire was built by an accumulative process. Its component parts were separately acquired, and were physically divided from each other and from the center of imperial power in Britain by expanses of ocean. To relatively unpopulated domains like Canada and Australia Britain exported colonists. To conquered territories already well populated, of which India was by far the most important, Britain exported garrison troops, administrators, merchants, and managers. The growth of the empire was accompanied by the growth of a caste system. Even "colonials" from Canada and Australia were long regarded as politically subordinate and socially uncouth. As for the peoples of India, Burma, and so on, even their aristocratic families were definitely subjects, not citizens.

Germany, France, Holland, Belgium, America, and

Japan, by the end of the century, all approximated to the British type in their relations with possessions overseas.

The Russian Empire was built by an incorporative process differing from the accumulative process. All of its holdings lay within one vast, unbroken expanse of land. Alaska, the one exception, was given up. Peoples were incorporated, as well as territories. The ordinary Russian was himself a subject, rather than a citizen. Non-Russian peoples were assimilated to the status of the Russians themselves. Ordinary people were held in subjection, but a part of the ruling class of each people was assimilated to the status of the Russian ruling class. The precedents for this kind of incorporation had been laid down long before. Centuries of interpenetration with nomadic peoples on the steppe frontier of European Russia had made class warfare and class politics as familiar as national warfare and politics to both Russians and non-Russians. When nomad khans had the upper hand, some of the Russian nobles became their vassals and continued as a ruling class; and though they were a subordinate part of the ruling class, the degree of subjection did not prevent intermarriage, which is all-important in welding a ruling class together. Then when the Russians in turn conquered the steppes and Siberia, they took part of the steppe nobility and tribal chieftains into their service, continued some of their privileges, and did not deny them intermarriage. There was even more intermarriage between subject Russians and subject non-Russians.

The differences between the British and Russian types of empire became of increasing importance as modern nationalism developed. Among the colonial subjects of the British many who would themselves have been high in the ruling class, had it not been for the British, were early leaders of nationalist movements for independence. In the Tsarist Empire, on the other hand, any form of revolution, including nationalist revolution, was bound to affect both Russians and non-Russians, who lived side by side, or intermingled with each other. In addition to what we think of as "Russian Asia" there were many minority "islands" of non-Russians scattered through the Russian population. Under such conditions, the majority of each non-Russian ruling class was bound to identify its interests with those of the Russian ruling class. Consequently the outcome of the Russian Revolution was determined, throughout the possessions of Russia in Asia, by a left-wing leadership which believed in revolution against its own ruling class as well as against the Russian state. There was thus a community of interest between the left-wing nationalists and the Bolsheviks, who were determined to destroy both the Tsarist state and the society that had supported it; whereas in a country like India, even British factory foremen and rank-and-file soldiers with non-Old-School-Tie accents identified themselves with their own ruling class against all "natives."

The Chinese Empire was the third great type, in spite of the fact that it was itself the victim of imperialist aggression. Its importance has been neglected simply because in modern times the Chinese state has been weak. The Chinese Empire was neither accumulative nor incorporative, but absorptive. The dominant characteristic in the territorial spread of the Chinese has been their willingness throughout history to accept as Chinese any barbarian who would drop his language and learn Chinese, wear Chinese clothes, farm like the Chinese, and accept the other conventions of being a Chinese. In earlier centuries this attitude was a source of untold strength to the Chinese: a great part of the nation is descended from barbarians absorbed into the Chinese state through being absorbed into the Chinese culture.

In the face of modern nationalism, however, this old Chinese strength has become a weakness. Peoples like the Mongols, the Tibetans, the Central Asian subjects of China, and even to a large extent the Chinese-speaking Moslems, reject a Chinese "equality" the price of which is abandonment of their own languages and other distinguishing cultural characteristics. Among the fatal mistakes of the Kuomintang, in its struggle with the Chinese Communists, was its attempt, even after the eleventh hour, to force the Chinese language on non-Chinese minorities, together with administrative subdivisions that prevented each minority from being represented in the government except as a subordinate part of a Chinese province.[1]

Changes in the distribution of power over the Far

[1] Compare Owen Lattimore, "The Inland Crossroads of Asia," in *Compass of the World*, edited by Hans Weigert and Vilhjalmur Stefansson, New York, 1944.

East in the second half of the nineteenth century were
effected by interaction between these three kinds of
empire. In this interaction it is not usually noted, but
certainly should be noted, that while China lost in
power to the other kinds of empire the Chinese in their
own empire gained in territory and in power over the
non-Chinese minorities.

The building of railways shows the double process
at work. Railways were in the first instance imposed
on China in the strategic and commercial interest of
foreign countries; but once built, they increased beyond all comparison with earlier periods the ability of
the Chinese to penetrate and make Chinese in population such frontier territories as the Manchurian provinces and Inner Mongolia. The Manchus were
drowned in their ancient homeland by the flooding
new population, and the Mongols were swept back
from thousands of square miles of territory in eastern
and southern Inner Mongolia. Other parts of China,
remote from the actual penetration of railways, were
also affected by the acceleration of economic and social change of which the railways were a part, and
which as a whole was driven forward by the economic
pressure of the West on China. One of the consequences was a speeding-up of the rate of absorption
of non-Chinese "tribal" minorities in the south and
west of China.

The external and internal aspects of the subordination of Asia in this age of empire must be understood
in relation to each other. In the external aspect the
predatory empires, spurred by trade rivalries and dif-

fering rates of industrialization, fought and maneu-
vered against each other; but while they could challenge each other in Europe, and sometimes in Asia
itself, Asia could not challenge them. When Britain
put down the Indian Mutiny, it was possible to go far
beyond the mere restoration of law and order. The
British were able to revise the entire administrative
system and to set up a new and more imperial one that
endured for many decades. When the West, after some
hesitation, decided not to let the Taiping Rebellion
in China take its course, but to uphold the Manchu
Dynasty, it was able to prolong the tenure of the dynasty for half a century.

When Britain, rounding out the northwestern frontier of India, and Russia, rounding out its conquests
in Inner Asia, decided not to go on sparring with each
other but each to recognize the other in its sphere of
activity, their decision stood. Britain and Russia decided the spheres of influence; countries like Persia
and Afghanistan were unable to assert the right, much
less to demonstrate the ability, to cross over from
the British sphere of influence into the Russian, even
when the line of division, as in Persia, ran right through
the country. A mere approximation toward agreement
between Britain and France, more tacit than explicit,
and motivated by their common interest in the face of
German rivalry, was enough to enable Siam to survive
as the only nominally independent country in Southeast Asia. China had to accept the way in which the
apportionment of power in Manchuria was repeatedly
changed by diplomatic representations, wars, and
treaties between the imperial powers.

In the internal aspect, on the other hand, Asia did
not remain "the unchanging East." Change was at
work below the level at which imperial control was
unchallengeable. In spite of its shaky sovereignty China
became more Chinese. Looking back from the present
we can see more clearly than contemporaries could
that in spite of all confusion it was in this period that
there originated an Indian nationalism and an Indian
mode of politics, and a Chinese nationalism and mode
of politics; and there were weaker but kindred stirrings
throughout the rest of Asia. Inevitably the nationalism
that developed under the lid of imperial rule and outside control was an anti-imperialist nationalism.

The difference between that time and this is that the
major and minor phenomena have changed places.
The primary, active force then at work was the pro-
jection of imperial power over Asia; the secondary,
reactive force was the beginning of nationalism among
the peoples and in the countries of Asia. The primary,
active force now is the dominant nationalism of Asia;
the secondary, reactive force is the effort to conserve
some of what remains of the old power of empire.
World instability then arose not out of Asia but out
of the incessant redistribution of power among the empires controlling Asia. Instability now arises out of the
fact that while Asia is in the main out of control from
the point of view of the West, it is not yet fully under
control from its own point of view. Nationalism is
dominant, but not completely free to act; national
policies are still clogged by the hampering remains of
external economic, strategic, and political control.

The Anglo-American Open Door Doctrine marks

the first clear phase of transition to a Far East out of control, and from rivalry between similar competitors to rivalry between competitors dissimilar from each other and hostile to each other in ideology, social and political structure, and economic operation. Before taking up this transition it is worth recalling the tone and temper of the age of empire, which began with an unworried acceptance of the changes and shifts of power, and ended with the disturbing fear of different kinds of power.

In the autumn of 1860 Raphael Pumpelly, a young American geologist and mining engineer, reached the end of the railway in Missouri. He pushed on to the Pacific and five years later completed his travels, truly formidable for that time, through Japan, China, Inner and Outer Mongolia, Siberia, and European Russia. The Russian railway did not then extend east of Nijnii-Novgorod.

Pumpelly was able to look out over the world, and over America's position in the world, from a point of advantage exceptional in his day. "If we look at a map of the world with reference to the inevitable future of the northern temperate zone," he wrote, "we shall find its greatest cultivable areas divided between two great sections of mankind, the Anglo-Saxon and the Sclavonic." (He even expected the Anglo-Saxons to dominate Latin America.)

Of Russia he went on to write that

When we consider the immense extent of this empire, and its capacity for population, wealth, and power, and then compare with it the small extent of western Europe, split up into small nationalities, with an overflowing population dependent on the east and west for its supply of food, the belief of the Pan-Slavist seems most prophetic; Russia, more than America, "hangs like a thunder cloud" over its western neighbors.

The expansion from the west and from the east to the opposite shores of the Pacific of two races and a civilization hitherto intimately connected with the Atlantic coasts, is already marking out for the Great ocean a most important part in the early future. Into this future history another element seems destined to enter; I mean the part that will be taken by the Chinese and Japanese peoples.

The immense resources of China in coal and iron and other minerals, in labor and the means of supporting life, and in the conformation of its surface, are elements which in the present and coming age cannot be idle. The utilizing of these resources cannot fail to be followed by the same results there as elsewhere, raising the nation by which they are developed to a position of authority in the world's affairs. There seems to me little doubt that this result will be accomplished by the Chinese people. In every direction we see in this race evidence of that vitality which has made of them a great nation. . . . This vitality is becoming important in a new and equally important direction: the Chinese are showing themselves to be essentially fitted to be colonizers, and as such they seem already to be resolving a great geographical problem. . . .[2]

Russian and American thinking were soon to come into contact. Several decades later a Russian traveler in the Far East named Klingen, startled by the extrovert

[2] Raphael Pumpelly, *Across America and Asia. Notes of a five years' journey around the world and of residence in Arizona, Japan and China*, fifth ed., revised, New York, 1871, especially pp. 1, 5, and 424-427.

self-assurance of the Americans he met, essayed a
sketch of Uncle Sam:

Indeed, the subject of the notorious Uncle Sam is not
exhausted by his advertising, and the way he fancies his
own greatness in his grandiose undertakings and his greatness in the not less grandiose contradictions of his
life. . . .
On the one hand, we have Uncle Sam encircled by a
halo of goodness and charity, sending across the ocean
whole boatloads of wheat to the starving Russians and
Hindus; on the other hand, he causes a ferocious struggle
for existence, and creates thousands of beggars and prole-
tarians.

The antiphonal account runs on: Uncle Sam is after
the Hawaiian Islands, Cuba, and the Philippines; Uncle
Sam sends Christian missionaries all over the world, but
he goes in for lynching "under the noses" of the
Senate and the House of Representatives. Above all,
the American represents the evolution of modern
capitalism. He has at his disposal fantastic resources
of steam and electricity. Under capitalism and technology, American life has become a "sport," in which
the rich and successful contend for the market, the
power of gold, the amassing of wealth, whilst the dull
masses fight for a piece of bread, "and in this merci-
less struggle for existence there is no place for the
weak and unsuccessful."

This premature Mr. Vyshinsky was a most respectable man in the Russia of his time. His book was published by the printing press of the *udel* or Imperial
Establishment of the Tsar. Moreover, while the Americans made him bristle, just as some Russians have al-

ways made some Americans bristle, he came to a generous conclusion:

> While it is true that for the ordinary onlooker Uncle Sam will always remain a two-faced Janus, an astonishing combination of great good and great evil, yet to him who wishes to penetrate more profoundly into the actual historical process that is going on beyond the ocean, America will undoubtedly present itself as the source of a bright future for all mankind — and I profoundly believe in the positive creative power of the North American people! [3]

These two witnesses of the age of empire were men who both reflected their own time very typically and in some ways foreshadowed our own time. Pumpelly, the American and the earlier of the two, accepted with equanimity some ideas of drastic change. He assumed the rise, between the expanding "Anglo-Saxon" and "Sclavonic" peoples, of a powerful Chinese nation. The prospect did not alarm him. He equated change with progress rather than with instability. He noted with approval the aptitude of the Chinese as industrial workers and the emergence of successfully competitive Chinese capitalists in Malaya and the Hawaiian Islands. The nearest that he came to an awareness of differing ideologies was in expressing his disapproval of the way in which the Chinese, in "our western territories," were

[3] I. Klingen, *Sredi patriarkhov zemledeliya narodov blizhnyago i dal'nyago vostoka (Egipet, Indiya, Tseilon, Kitai i Yaponiya).* Chast' III, Kitai. Among the patriarchs of agriculture of the peoples of the Near and Far East (Egypt, India, Ceylon, China, and Japan). Part III, China, pp. 150–153. St. Petersburg, 1899.

treated "worse than dogs"; he tentatively approved of intermarriage, because of "the danger of the formation of caste if such a mixture does not take place." [4]

Klingen, the Russian, coming at the very end of the period, showed the troubled dawn of ideological hostility. He was irritated by the vulgar American assumption that money is what creates power. With the authoritarian and feudal tradition of Russia behind him, his feeling was that power should create money. He used the words "capitalist" and "proletariat" with recognizable distaste. The way in which capitalists create a proletariat disturbs status; and it was in a society of status that he felt at home. One can almost write for him, between the lines, a statement that if only the American capitalist were subject to regulation through the granting of licences or concessions by a higher political authority, he would be socially acceptable. His feeling for authority, however, also constrained him to respect power, once in existence, no matter what its origin, and thus in the end he reconciled himself to America with the reflection that "fortunately, capitalism does not by a long way exhaust the inner significance of the life of the great transoceanic republic," so that America could still "present itself as the source of a bright future for all mankind." [5]

Up to the time of the Open Door Doctrine the unceasing redistribution of power in Europe and over Asia was conducted under conventions accepted by all

[4] Pumpelly, p. 426.
[5] Klingen, p. 153.

the competitors. Countries competed with each other in seizing ports and bases and controlling lines of communication and access to new, unexploited territories. If the rivalry led to war, the winner acquired immediate rewards in the form of indemnities and annexations. The loser paid an indemnity and ceded territory, or bases, or priority of access to a country that might be conquered and made into a colony, but was not debarred from recovery and re-entry into competition. No Carthaginian peace terms were imposed; the rules of the game were observed, and the game went on.

The Open Door Doctrine partially succeeded in changing the rules of the game, because the nature of the game was changing. It was the stop-Russia doctrine of its day, at least on the British side, and it is curious how practically all mention of its origin as a policy to "contain" Russian expansion has dropped out of recent historical writing. Lord Charles Beresford, who in the winter of 1898–1899 toured China on behalf of the Associated Chambers of Commerce of Great Britain, and then went on to America to advocate the adoption of the Open Door, was perfectly plain-spoken. In *The Break-Up of China*, the book he wrote describing his mission, he referred on page after page to the danger that Russian occupation of Chinese territory might put an end to the opportunities for merchants of other countries.[6]

[6] Lord Charles Beresford, *The Break-Up of China*, New York, 1899. It is worth notice in passing that the doughty Beresford was a bit of a Colonel Blimp. Winston Churchill described him as "one of those orators who, before they get

In his book *China and America*, Mr. Foster Rhea Dulles, the American historian who has most clearly dealt with the Russian aspect of the origin of the Open Door, cites the American press of 1898 as interpreting the situation to mean that "the real danger in the Chinese situation came from Russia, whose persistent advance in Manchuria appeared to foreshadow imperialistic control over all north China." He adds that Secretary of State John Hay's objective "was to thwart discrimination against American trade from any quarter," whereas "Great Britain had perhaps hoped to draw the United States into a common policy primarily directed against Russia." [7] But while Hay was not ready to commit America to a policy directed more against Russia than against other rivals in China, other Americans were beginning to think of Russia uneasily. Henry Adams, friend of John Hay and the State Department "insiders," was one of those who were alarmed by the "glacier"-like advance of Russia on China.[8]

The Open Door formula brought into being in fact, though not by specific declaration, a league of countries with maritime access to the trade of the

---

up, do not know what they are going to say; when they are speaking, do not know what they are saying; and, when they have sat down, do not know what they have said." — "Sparks from the Anvil," *Atlantic Monthly*, Boston, January 1949, p. 25.

[7] Foster Rhea Dulles, *China and America*, Princeton, 1946, pp. 106 and 110.

[8] Henry Adams, *The Education of Henry Adams*, 1918; cited from Boston edition of 1927, p. 440.

Far East, to maintain conditions under which they could compete with each other and could enjoin Russia, which alone had easy, commercially exploitable access to China by land, to observe those conditions. In order to make the policy effective it was necessary to renounce annexations, because if annexations were allowed, Russia, which could annex contiguous territories and incorporate them with the home domain, had an advantage of position that would make the competition of the others futile. To put it in another way, the Open Door rewrote the rules of the game in such a way as to try to make Russia, in spite of having a land frontier with China longer than the American-Canadian frontier, act as nearly as possible as if it had access to China only by sea.

Japan was the most enthusiastic of all the countries that accepted the Open Door notes. Japan was at the time still under "unequal treaty" disabilities, as was China; but Japan had also already fought a successful imperialist war against China, had been deprived of part of the spoils of war by Russia (with the backing of France and Germany), and was in a position to accept bids for support as a sentinel against Russian expansion. A few years later, with Britain neutral on her side (in the Irish sense of the word "neutral") and the United States certainly not neutral against her, Japan defeated Russia.

Japan then began to show an ambivalent ability to be both a part of the old system of keeping Asia under control and a part of the new process that eventually resulted in Asia's becoming out of control. As the most permanently anti-Russian of the maritime powers, Japan was essential to the working of the Open Door system. As a power within Asia, and so close to the mainland of Asia as to have almost the same kind of contiguity enjoyed by Russia, Japan sabotaged the Open Door. To the extent that support against Russia was useful, Japan worked with the Open Door powers; but step by step, as Japanese control was expanded over Manchuria and into North China, commercial opportunities and the exploitation of all resources were monopolized in favor of Japan and to the exclusion of other Open Door powers.

This ambivalence of Japanese policy, which goes with Japan's geographical position, should not be overlooked now when it is so fashionable to think of Japan as a trustworthy ally. No necessity ties Japan down to be permanently an ally in Asia of powers outside of Asia. Nothing guarantees America against the possibility that while some Japanese demand American help against "Communist imperialism," other Japanese, who could easily become a majority, may negotiate for an understanding with China, and through China with Russia, as an offset against "American imperialism." The propaganda of "Asia for the Asiatics" was not silenced by Japan's defeat in the war. It is still a good line of propaganda, though it falls now on different ears, or ears differently attuned.

The next phase in the passage of Asia from being under control to being out of control was marked by the Chinese Revolution of 1911. At the time of the Taiping Rebellion, the Western powers had been able

to salvage the Manchu Dynasty. By 1911, not only
was it impossible to salvage the dynasty; even the
nomination of Yuan Shih-k'ai as a "strong man" to
maintain the security of loans and investments was far
from successful. The Western formula for a strong
man called for a man strong enough to carry out policies urgently demanded by foreign diplomats, but not
quite strong enough to defy foreign control. The
measure of the changes going on in Asia was that by
the time of the Chinese Revolution a man not quite
strong enough to defy the special interests of foreign
countries was also not quite strong enough to be a
dictator in China.[9] In the same way it was just not in
the cards that Chiang Kai-shek could be made dictator
of China after the defeat of Japan, when the major
political demand all over China was for wider representative government.

The third phase of transition was the Russian Revolution, which brought about new alignments in both
the West and Asia. With the Russian Revolution, the
old rules of the game of international relations completely broke down, both in war and in peace. Here
was a country thoroughly defeated, which instead of
acknowledging defeat according to the accepted conventions began a new kind of warfare. In war between

[9] In this connection a professorial colleague of mine once
remarked that the recommendation of Professor Frank J.
Goodnow of Johns Hopkins University which encouraged
Yuan Shih-k'ai to try to make himself Emperor was not
wrong because it was morally wrong. It was wrong because
by then it was "just not in the cards" for any man to make
himself, or be made, Emperor of China.

imperial powers, the use of colonial troops is considered acceptable. Both Indian and African troops have fought splendidly in Europe. But there is no form of appeal by which one imperial power can win over, in large numbers, the colonial troops of another imperial power. Germany tried unsuccessfully to find such an appeal in the First World War. Revolutionary Russia succeeded, by declaring a war of ideas, and wherever possible of arms, on behalf of all colonial subjects against all imperial rulers.

The development in Asia that responded to the Russian Revolution was the realization that the ranks of the imperial powers now showed a gap, and that weak countries and immature political movements could now take advantage of a new kind of irreconcilable quarrel among great powers. Russia had been one of the greatest of the empires. The fact that such an empire could not only be defeated in war but subverted by an internal, antimonarchic revolution roused a new vigor in the nationalism of all subject peoples and half-subject peoples like the Chinese. Up to this time, the best that a weak country like China could do was to try to play great powers against each other. But the rival interests of the great powers were also similar interests. For this reason Chinese exploitation of their rivalry could never achieve more than a partial success; at this point similarity of interest invariably superseded rivalry of interest, and China was confronted once more with united policies and united demands.

The hostility between Russia and the other great

powers was not of this reconcilable kind. Russia was the only great power that showed unlimited willingness to defy and considerable ability to defy successfully the very countries that exercised control or rule over countries like China, India, and the rest of Asia. Those of the capitalist countries that consider themselves democratic, and base their political appeal on democracy, have always been the most reluctant to admit that this characteristic of Russia is the basic reason why colonial and subject peoples do not make reliable anti-Russian allies.

Wherever Russian and Communist propaganda can be traced, Russian methods of using political movements in weak and dependent countries to throw great powers off balance and to hamper their political maneuvers have been studied. The importance of making such studies has led to neglect in studying the answering process in Asia: the way in which nationalist movements all over Asia exploit — and the word "exploit" is not too strong — the existence of Russia. As long as such movements, even when they are non-Communist, can exploit the existence of Russia in their struggle against Britain, France, or Holland, they have a vested interest in the continued existence of a strong Russia.

The fact that in Russia one of the world's great imperial governments had collapsed was the first and most powerful Russian propaganda. It is significant that in China Sun Yat-sen showed interest in the Russian Revolution before the new Soviet Government showed interest in him. Chou En-lai, a Chinese intellectual living in France, jumped from the Social Demo-

cratic Second International to the Communist Third
International because he appreciated that the mere existence of a revolutionary Russia made it possible to
strike out for China's emancipation in new and more
effective ways. Chu Teh, a professional soldier who
had gone to Germany to study military organization
because, like many Chinese, he considered that Germany, even though defeated in the First World War,
had shown superior military skill, turned instead to
Communism, because as a soldier he was convinced
that the Bolsheviks, in the Russian civil war and in re-
sisting the intervention of the great powers, had developed the kinds of military skill most suited to China.
Similarly in India Nehru, without benefit of Russian
prompting, began a careful study of the founders and
leaders of world Communism, even though he never
became a Communist himself. All of these are famous
names; there are many others, all over Asia, whose
names are less famous.

The fourth phase of transition was dominated by
Japan's aggressions. During this phase it became plain
that Asia had passed out of control in two ways. In the
first place, Japan itself, maneuvering from a position
within Asia and between Russia and the great capitalist
powers, could not be made to abide by the rules of a
game which theoretically required all capitalist nations
with interests in Asia to help each other exclude Russia from the Far East, but not to exclude each other
from the competitive market. Japan's capitalists, as
well as Japan's militarists, took aid from other countries for the avowed purpose of strengthening them-

selves against Russia, but made their own nonaggression pact with Russia when it suited them, and attacked those countries with which they were supposed to have the most fundamental interests in common. In the second place, while Japan thus proved itself out of control from the point of view of the West, the mainland of Asia, and especially the massive bulk of China, proved to be out of control from the point of view of Japan.

The phases of transition were completed with the end of the war. The uncontrollability of Asia is now nearing its full development. The characteristics of this new period must be carefully studied. In world politics, they now constitute an important part of the new rules of the game. They are binding rules. We do not like the way they were drawn up, but ever since the war we have been learning, in the most hard and disagreeable way, that we are in no position to play the game against the rules.

CHAPTER III

LEGACY OF WAR

CURRENT American thinking about the power situation resulting from World War II starts from the assumption that America and Russia, in that order, have become the two most powerful countries in the world — so powerful that they can and must divide the world between them. Any part of the world that America cannot enclose within a steel ring, the argument runs, will be enclosed by Russia behind an iron curtain. The trouble with this thinking is that it does not begin at the beginning. It is not the *absolute* but the *relative* power of both America and Russia that counts. Both countries have grown in relative power because of the enormous power lost by Germany and Japan, and the almost equally great power lost by Britain, France, and, in the colonial world, Holland. Some of the power lost by these countries has been transferred directly to America and Russia, with America acquiring far more than Russia; but much of it has not.

This unredistributed power is as important and critical in Asia today as is the power of America or Russia. Some of it may come into American or Russian hands. In China, India, and colonial Asia, however, most of it has already been taken by parties and movements which vary in their ideas of social and economic revolution, but are alike in their intense nationalism. All parties in these countries, whatever the political orientation of their party members, are subject to an unceasing nationalistic pressure from the millions of their countrymen who are not members of any party, but do feel themselves to be part of the forward drive of a tremendous nationalist movement.

The victories of Japan in the first two years after Pearl Harbor destroyed the old specifications on which estimates of power in Asia were based. They left us with an Asia out of control: but not all parts of Asia are out of control to the same degree, and therefore conflicting policies in Asia stem from conflicting estimates of the key factors that constitute power. What we are finding out, through these conflicts of policy, is that the ability to defeat Japan did not confer on the victor nations either the ability to undo what Japan had done successfully or the ability to complete what Japan had not succeeded in completing.

What Japan did do successfully was to destroy the nineteenth-century structure of colonial empire in Asia. As long as colonial rule was a going concern, nationalism and rebellion could be dealt with by police action. Key points, lines of communication, and control of the press and radio were in the hands of the rulers. The shipping out of colonial products and the shipping in of capital and consumer goods were running along profitably. Influential individuals and sometimes whole classes among the subject peoples hesitated to risk too much in supporting the cause of political freedom, because they feared economic losses in the period of transition. The leadership of nationalism was divided, and support for it was uneven.

Not a single territory that had been occupied by the Japanese during the war could be taken back as a going concern. Colonial peoples who had never been armed before had got possession of arms. They controlled parts of the territories. They controlled newspaper and radio facilities. Under the Japanese, some of those who had been rich and powerful had lost money or prestige, or both. New men had become influential. Even those who thought it to their own interest to come to terms again with the British, or the French or Dutch, saw no reason for handing back to their former rulers exactly the kind of power that they had had before. They wanted to bargain, and to secure better terms for themselves. In every case, therefore, the would-be returning rulers had to make a separate calculation: could they get away with a reconquest, or would they have to negotiate, or could they mix force and negotiation in different proportions?

Both in reacting emotionally to moral issues and in making what we think are hardheaded decisions in power politics, Americans are the most unrealistic political thinkers in the world. Until we get some of the illusions shaken out of us, we are certain to go on stumbling into the same kind of mess that we stumbled into in China in 1948. The year 1949 is likely to shake a good many illusions out of us. The question is whether enough will be shaken out, in time.

One of our grand illusions is that colonial issues are essentially moral issues, not issues of power. We assume that we have been "good" to the Filipinos, while the European powers have not been "good," or not "good" enough, to their subjects in Asia. The truth is that the basic colonial relationship is one of power. In Indonesia, the basic issue to be settled is not whether the Dutch were as good or generous to the Indonesians as they ought to have been. The issue is one of power. The Dutch did not have the power to hold Indonesia against the Japanese. They did not have the power to take it back from the Japanese. A British force landed to receive the Japanese surrender and held on long enough to shoehorn the Dutch back in. The Dutch still have no real power of their own. When they moved to crush Indonesian nationalism in December 1948, their calculation was based on the assumption that they had America backed into a corner. Because of the priority given by American policy to a Western Union of Holland, Belgium, France, Luxemburg, and Britain, to form the nucleus of a North Atlantic Pact, they reasoned that America would continue to pour Marshall Plan aid into Holland, enabling Holland to transfer strength to Indonesia and to hang onto sources of strategic supplies like oil, rubber, and tin. The upshot now turns on whether this mockingly disguised Dutch use of American subsidy for colonial conquest, obtained by blackmail, will be enough to do the job, or whether Indonesian guerrilla warfare will be able to make Chiang Kai-sheks of the Dutch.

The American illusion about the moral nature of the

colonial relationship is largely an outgrowth of our connection with the Philippines. But our relationship with the Philippines has been abnormal, not normal, in the history of colonial rule. Unlike any colony-owning European country, we had our main raw material resources in our homeland. Neither the moral suasion of the Filipinos nor their ability to rebel prevailed on us to grant them their independence. The deciding influence was the lobbying of American interests which wished to exclude Philippine products from America, or to diminish and regulate the amount imported by applying tariffs and quotas, which could only be done if the Philippines were independent. Such a policy looked better, of course, when garnished with moral arguments in favor of independence, and was therefore so presented to the public.

In European countries that owned colonies the powerful influences were always those that wished to import colonial products, or to control them on the world market, not those that wished to exclude them. Naturally, they have always adorned the policy of holding onto colonial rule by laying on themselves the "moral obligation" not to grant independence before their subjects are "fit" for it. The truth is, therefore, that when Americans talk about the moral obligation to grant as much independence as possible and to do it as soon as possible, and when Europeans talk about the moral obligation not to turn their subjects loose prematurely, they are talking at cross-purposes. No European country has yet granted independence or any degree of self-government to any of its colonial subjects except when it was compelled to admit that it was no longer able to impose the sanction of force.

British policy shows how the difference between open rebellion and negotiation in advance of open rebellion is determined by the ruling power's estimate of its own strength.

Even India, though not occupied by the Japanese, could no longer be treated as a colonial "going concern." Thousands of Indian war veterans were returning to India from Africa, Europe, and the Near East at the same time that thousands of British war veterans wanted nothing except to go home. Nationalist morale among Indian servicemen was high. Imperialist morale among British servicemen was low. There were no Churchills in the uniform of private soldiers. Revolt in India had barely been averted during the war. Revolt after the war could neither have been prevented by force nor put down by force if it had broken out. In the case of India and Pakistan the British granted dominion status, including the option of full independence, because they calculated that if they hung on until rebellion broke out, they would lose more than if they negotiated in time. By negotiating, they were able to salvage a major portion of their economic interests, including control over the repayment of their own huge sterling debt to India. In the case of Malaya, they calculated that if rebellion broke out, they would be able to crush it.

Britain, as the greatest of the colonial empires, also illustrates the range of policy from negotiation on a footing of full equality to attempted reconquest. In

India, Pakistan, and Ceylon dominion status was negotiated, and in Burma full independence. Britain in
Malaya, however, just as Holland in Indonesia and
France in Indo-China, has not yet been willing to give
up as much as will eventually have to be given up. The
only thing that is yet clear in these countries, from the
imperial point of view, is that the best that can be
hoped for is a partially successful salvage operation.
Some interests may yet be saved. The ruling interest
itself cannot be saved.

The fact that Japan did not succeed in China is as
important as the fact that Japan did succeed in over-
running all of colonial Asia except India and Ceylon.
The control over China that Japan failed to make good
cannot now be asserted by any other country. It is true
that there are differences of opinion about whether
Russia might succeed; but there can be no differences
of opinion about America. Between August 1945 and
the end of 1948 we spent two billion dollars (unoffi-
cial estimates run much higher) on an extensive field
test to demonstrate that America cannot control China.

American illusions about the scope of power politics
in China contrast with the American illusion that a
difference in moral attitude is what distinguishes the
American policy in the Philippines from the colonial
policies of European countries. Ever since the defeat
of Japan, American discussion of the fate of China has
harped on the idea that China is a field of power which
should be "preventively" occupied by the United
States in order to keep Russia out; otherwise, China
will either have to be divided between America and

Russia, or it will be occupied by Russia to the detriment of America. The truth is that the places that China and colonial Asia hold in American thought should be reversed. In determining the future of China, moral attitude will take precedence over power politics. In determining the future of colonial Asia, power politics will take precedence over moral attitude.

In the colonial countries the structure of European imperial power proved to be so flimsy when attacked by Japan that the question of relative superiority between European and Japanese moral attitudes never really arose. The question in colonial Asia now is whether the nationalist movements have the power to get rid of what remains of European power, or whether the European countries have enough power to hang onto what remains of their rule. When further fighting has made it possible to measure power more accurately, the question of moral attitudes will come to the fore and be decisive; but not until then.

In China, on the other hand, the long and bloody Japanese attempt at conquest proved that Japan did not have the kind of power that was able to settle Chinese issues. The grandiose and disastrous American attempt to determine the character and outcome of the Chinese civil war then proved that America does not have the kind of power that can settle Chinese issues. There remains Russia. It is extremely doubtful that Russia, faced with unsettled issues in Europe, could invade China with several million men, as Japan did. Nor can Russia bring to bear on China the kind of power with which America experimented unsuccessfully. The American expenditure of from two to four billion dollars included both military and economic aid to Chiang Kai-shek. Both forms of aid represented the surplus factory output of the most heavily industrialized country in the world. Russia, and especially Asiatic Russia, east of the Urals, does not have that kind of surplus.

Russia therefore cannot use on China either the kind of power that was used by Japan or the kind that was used by America. There remains only political infiltration, or persuasion, which is a moral question. If the Russians fail in this approach, there is no reason to believe that they can fall back on power politics. There is every reason to believe that China is beyond the power-politics control of Russia, as it is beyond the power-politics coercion of Japan and America.

The question of the redistribution of power has two aspects, one of which is usually overlooked. When a country suddenly acquires greatly increased power, the fact stands out. Ever since 1945, America and Russia have loomed like giants over the world. Beginning with 1948, the less obvious aspect of power began to play its part in power politics: that aspect is the fact that all power, even the greatest, has its limits. In 1949, the defining of the limits of power has become the most sensitive test of statesmanship. Where runs the line beyond which the expansive power of Russia diminishes rapidly? What part of the power formerly held by Germany, Japan, Britain, France, and Holland has America not inherited?

Both the redistribution of power and the limits of

power stand out clearly on the map. Around and across Asia, from the Mediterranean to the Pacific, two frontiers of power are strung, like two loops of a necklace. The lower loop is attached at its western end to Greece. It runs through Turkey, the Arab states, Iran, and Afghanistan; then drops below India to Malaya and Indonesia, and up through the Philippines and Taiwan (Formosa) to Okinawa and Japan. The upper loop runs from the Balkan frontier of Greece along the Soviet frontiers of Turkey, Iran, Afghanistan, and Sinkiang (Chinese Central Asia). It then drops below Mongolia, thus including the Mongolian People's Republic as a Soviet satellite, and around the Northeastern Provinces of China (Manchuria) to Korea.

The lower loop defines what is left of the structure of imperial rule and control in Asia. It shows that the European powers, and America as their partial heir, hold only a doubtful control of territories in Asia. All that they really hold is a string of bases around the rim of Asia. They have fallen back to the footholds and toeholds from which the European marauders and adventurers of the sixteenth and early seventeenth centuries began their empire building. Most of the vast possessions and spheres of influence that were consolidated in the eighteenth and nineteenth centuries have been lost. Both Europe and America are on the outside, looking in.

Another fact stares at us from the map. The ruins of empire are least shaky where they are anchored at points that can be considered primarily as bases, and there are very few of these left: Aden, Singapore,

Hong Kong. Wherever the frontier of power touches populated territory, people — which means politics — have become more important than garrisons. Greece is a doubtful stronghold. It is a stronghold in which the garrison is besieged by the populace. The Arab states are not strongholds. Until recently, they had no politics except the politics of kings and sheiks who were the personal feudatories of Great Britain. Small grants from the British Exchequer and small consignments of rifles and machine guns were enough to regulate their power so that each was strong enough to keep his people in subordination while none was strong enough to unite an Arab nation. Arab armies were personal armies, each bound to its king or emir by tribal, feudal, or mercenary loyalty. As of 1949, there is not a single Arab army that is not capable of overthrowing its ruler and opening a new phase of nationalist politics.

Iran and Afganistan are not strongholds. In both countries, the politics of nationalism, of peoples and parties, have already begun to supersede the politics of personal and feudal rulers. Pakistan and India are out of control. In both countries, Europeans and Americans who have money to invest or goods to sell can make deals that are profitable for individuals and corporations; but neither the British nor the American government can line up economic control, still less political control, and least of all strategic control. The same is true of Burma. Of the old Indian Empire, the island of Ceylon alone is likely to remain a controllable satellite for a few years.

In Malaya, Indonesia, and Indo-China the British,

Dutch, and French were once the forerunners of expanding empire. Now they are fighting rear-guard actions in shrinking empires. The Republic of the Philippines is not a dependable American satellite. The politics of nationalism inside the country are becoming dominant over the politics of the personal agents of American interests. In less than two years, the military installations granted to America when the Philippines assumed independence in 1946 will virtually be besieged strongholds, looking out on a sullen population entirely undependable as an instrument of American power politics.

Taiwan, if American policy should make the mistake of trying to protect there a refugee government from the mainland of China, will not be a secure base. Its people detest the Kuomintang and Chiang Kai-shek as the president to whom they appealed in vain to stop the plundering of the Kuomintang when China recovered Taiwan from Japanese rule. Even their nationalist loyalty to China was shaken by the excesses and cruelties of the greedy Kuomintang carpetbaggers who took over the island: there was a widespread desire to be taken over as an American protectorate. For this very reason, if America were to turn Taiwan into a combined base for the American Navy and refuge for a Kuomintang government expelled from China, anti-American feeling would develop rapidly and there would be a new, Communist-tinged nationalism once more demanding reunion with China.

Even Japan is not a secure American base. There are too many Japanese. An American dole can keep them alive, but not in comfort or dignity. Their permanent sources of raw materials and permanent markets lie in Asia, not in America or Europe. They must eventually come to terms with Asia. If Asia is out of control, and America cannot guarantee them access, then there will be an inevitable demand that Japan break away from America in order to come to terms with Asia. This demand will begin to show itself clearly in Japanese politics in 1949, and will develop with disconcerting rapidity in the next year or two.

In contrast with the shaky southern frontier around Asia, the Soviet frontier across Asia is firm. It is certainly not a retreating frontier. What troubles the foreign offices and strategic planners of Europe and America is the possibility that it may be an advancing frontier.

It is a mistake to try to answer this question by looking only at the map of Asia. The frontiers of Russian power have expanded up to the ruins of empire in Europe as well as in Asia. Hitler's empire in Europe was not called colonial, but it was colonial in fact. His colonies lay in Eastern Europe, the valley of the Danube, and the Balkans. His subject peoples functioned like the subjects of any colonial empire in Africa or Asia. In standard of living and social and political status they were classified below the Germans. Some of them were recruited as troops, but only as auxiliary troops. They suffered the casualties of battle, but the Germans took the rewards of victory, as long as victories continued. In their "colonial" territories in Eastern Europe the Germans, as did the British in India, manipulated the economic exchange. In the main, Eastern Europe produced food and raw materials for Germany and got machinery and consumer goods from Germany. Industrialization was carefully watched, and kept subordinate to the key processes of industry in Germany.

In the postwar redistribution of world power, therefore, in Europe as in Asia, the Russian expansion extends into the colonial domains of defeated, weakened, or retreating empires, while American expansion has resulted in hegemony over the industrial and highly developed centers which formerly controlled empires. In defining the limits of power, America faces the fact that it is enormously expensive to reconstruct highly developed economic structures which were originally adapted to the intake of colonial economic tribute. The risky and makeshift aspect of Marshall Plan economics is that, of necessity, one of its activities is to supply European countries, at high dollar cost which they cannot control, with the kinds of raw material which they used to obtain from their colonial possessions at low costs in currencies which they themselves controlled. America has been finding out that the rump of an empire, without the body of its imperial possessions, makes a defective instrument of power.

Russia, on the other hand, has been finding out that there are also limits to its new expansion of power which, though geographically vast, represents principally access to the colonial possessions of dismembered empires — without their power-centers of highly developed industry and technology. The Russian economy is not so constructed that it can take over the possessions of other empires and exploit them as other empires did. Its new power, therefore, does not mean the transfer to Russia of either the exact quantities or the exact kinds of power that other empires had. America, which suffered no devastation in the war, had a steel production, in 1948, of almost 90,000,000 tons. Russian steel production for the same year was estimated at under 20,000,000 tons; and a high proportion of this cannot be allocated to the development of marginal or satellite territories, because it must go into the repair of the terrible war devastation that Russia suffered.

Comparison between the Russian and the American situation shows that Russia has acquired control of, or access to, enormous exploitable areas, but has not taken over, from those who formerly exploited them, the same kind of ability to exploit. America has acquired an immensely increased ability to exploit, but has access to a far smaller total territory to exploit than did the great empires whose power has so largely passed into American hands.

This comparison indicates that there is a third quotient of power to be considered: that which was once enjoyed by the great powers not only in their own colonial possessions but in countries like China and the countries of Eastern Europe, but has not yet passed into the hands of either America or Russia, and instead of passing into their hands may remain in the possession of peoples once subject or subordinate. This third quotient of power is something that has much more vigor than the vague and listless "third force" of Europe. The third force in Europe is led by a hesitant and dwindling fraction of the middle class and leads a harried life between the revival of big business interests which always put money above patriotism, and the growth of a tough, proletarian, class-conscious, and aggressive Communism and left-wing socialism that is not so much disloyal to old standards of patriotism as utterly contemptuous of them. The "third quotient" of power is an utterly different phenomenon. It is a heritage that has fallen to whole peoples, rather than to classes. These peoples are infused with a vigorous nationalist loyalty that the upper classes of Western Europe no longer have and the proletariat of Western Europe does not want; because throughout Western Europe international class loyalties have either superseded old national loyalties or are fast superseding them.

There is a field for the political development of the third quotient of power in Eastern Europe. There is another in Latin America. There will be a third in Africa, as nationalism begins to evolve there. But the main field lies in Asia: in that part of Asia between the Soviet land frontier and the rim of coastal and island bases held by America and the European powers, which according to old strategic standards and political conventions is out of control. It is in this field that there is a new chapter in the history of nationalism and revolution to be studied.

CHAPTER IV

NATIONALISM AND REVOLUTION

In an Asia that is out of control two forces are at work — nationalism and revolution. Of these two, nationalism is the more elemental force. To a large extent, nationalism is "revolutionary" simply because the change is from subjection to independence and from arbitrary government by imposed authority to forms of government that are made possible only by "the consent of the governed" and at least the crude beginnings of representative government. For Asia, these changes are so sudden and so great that they exceed the pace of evolution and can only be called revolutionary.

The policies in Asia of powers that stand outside of Asia can no longer control these developments, but they can still influence them. Since these limitations apply to Russian policy as well as to American policy and to the policies of the European empires, the fact that the changes being brought about by nationalism in Asia are of necessity revolutionary does not mean that, in passing out of the control of America and Europe, they have passed wholly under the control of Russia. What we do have to contend with, however, is the fact that the Russians are professional revolutionaries. Unless we can learn to match the Russians in professional skill in the art of influencing revolutions which we cannot control, the advantage will lie with them.

Russian policy throughout the world consists of something more than agile, catlike pounces on opportune mice that happen to pop out of decaying political structures. It is based on a formidable combination of the Communist theory of how history unfolds, phase by phase, and those methods which the existing resources of the Soviet state enable it to use whenever a theoretical phase has ceased to be theoretical and has become an actual situation.

In Communist theory, human history is an unceasing conflict of social classes, in which a double process of growth and decay is always going on. The ruling class, even when it appears to be in complete control, carries within itself the seeds of decay. Some other class is gathering strength and growing, and will eventually overthrow it. "Revolution" is what happens when the growing class shoulders the decaying class aside and takes its place. "Progress" is a relative concept. In the history of society, feudalism is considered "progressive" relative to slave-owning, but "reactionary" relative to the capitalism that eventually displaced feudalism. It is this kind of historical relativity that enables the Russians to exalt a dead Peter the Great, though they would regard a live one with horror.

According to this theory, to be "progressive" in politics means to be on the side of that which is coming up and against that which is going down. "A rising

class, though yet relatively weak, is a better bet politically than one which has had its rise and, though still
relatively powerful, is beginning to decline. Hence,
according to Stalin, the Marxists were right in basing
their policy on the proletariat even in Russia in the
1880's, because it was evolving as a class, while the
peasantry, though in the enormous majority, was declining as a class." [1]

The Soviet method, following this Communist theory, is to go into action whenever it looks as though a
"step forward" can be taken. A step forward, according to this combination of theory and method, is always a step forward, even when it does not reach all
the way to control of the state by Communists. In the
1920's Russia was delighted to help Sun Yat-sen in
China, even though Sun Yat-sen specifically made the
reservation that "the communistic order, or even the
Soviet system, cannot actually be introduced into
China because there do not exist the conditions for
the successful establishment of either communism or
Sovietism." From the Russian point of view, anything
that Sun Yat-sen could do to weaken the hold of the
foreign powers over China, and the war lords within
China, was "progressive."

When Chiang Kai-shek turned against the Communists and started a civil war to exterminate them, the

[1] Quoted from an article by "Historicus" on "Stalin on
Revolution," in *Foreign Affairs*, New York, January 1949.
This article brings together the most valuable original cita-
tions published in America for many years to illustrate the
Soviet theory of opportunity and action.

Russians were of course disappointed. But this defeat they regarded as only a relative defeat. In spite of their virulent propaganda against him, they recognized that Chiang Kai-shek's government was better able to defend China against encroachment than the war-lord governments that preceded it. Therefore when he began to resist Japan, they gave him arms — not because they liked him, but because they themselves feared Japan. The help given him before Russia itself was invaded in 1941 was greater than the help from either America or Britain before Pearl Harbor. When, during the war, Chiang's troops clashed with those of the Chinese Communists, the Russians turned their propaganda against him in reproof (just as the American press also reacted in alarm); but even in these crises they made no effort to supply arms to the Chinese Communists.

Stalin quotes from Lenin a "fundamental law of revolution" indicating the point at which a theoretical phase becomes an actual situation, in which the Soviet state can go into action, using whatever methods are practical at the time. This definition is so close to being a description of Asia today, out of the control or slipping out of the control both of the old empires and of America's vast postwar expansion of power, that it must give the men in the Kremlin the feeling of knowing exactly what is happening:

> For revolution it is not enough that the exploited and oppressed masses should feel the impossibility of living in the old way and demand change; for revolution it is necessary that the exploiters should not be able to live and

rule in the old way. Only when the *"lower classes"* *do not want* the old way and when the "upper classes" *cannot carry on in the old way* — only then can revolution conquer.[2]

We even have Stalin's own formula, written down in 1921 but first published only in 1947, defining "the arrival of the moment for revolutionary outbreaks." While the Lenin definition reads like an accurate prophecy of an Asia out of control, the Stalin formula is so electrifyingly exact a description of the situation in China that it should be studied with cautious respect both in analyzing the present debacle of American policy in China and in attempting to forecast future relations between China and Russia. The opportunity, says Stalin, comes:

When the revolutionary mood of the masses . . . brims over and our slogans for action and directives lag behind the movement of the masses. . . . When uncertainty and confusion, disintegration and dissolution in the adversary's camp have reached the highest point . . . when the so-called neutral elements, all that mass of many millions of city and village petty bourgeoisie, begin definitely to turn away from the adversary . . . and seeks alliance with the proletariat.[3]

When Russians read this kind of statement, they are convinced of the foresight and wisdom of their leaders. They have the feeling that their country and their cause are going forward on the tide of history. Ameri-

[2] "Historicus," quoting Stalin's quotation of Lenin, in the article in *Foreign Affairs* already cited. Italics in original.
[3] *Ibid.*

cans, on the other hand, should not overlook a very interesting point: Russians and Communists cannot prove that these theories are right. Only we can prove that. Only we can "prove" that the society which claims the freedoms that we claim has lost its political know-how, can no longer "carry on in the old way," and has lost the knack of guiding change and growth into evolutionary, democratic channels.

These glimpses into the way in which Soviet policy correlates its methods of exploiting opportunities with its theory of how opportunities come about are enough to show, however, that those who plan and carry out American policy will fall into a trap if they think that what is required of them is a decision between "Europe first" and "Asia first." In 1946, 1947, and 1948 Europe fitted the combined specifications of the Communist theory of what constitutes an opportunity and the methods available to the Soviet state for exploiting an opportunity better than Asia. In 1949 Asia fits the specifications better than Europe. But both then and now the situations in Europe and in Asia have never ceased to interact on each other.

What was falling from 1946 to 1948 was the old system of German imperial domination over Eastern Europe. America, Britain, and France were able to stop Russia from taking over Germany in addition to Germany's old "colonial" empire because the expansion of American power more than matched the expansion of Russian power. But they were unable to take over control to their own satisfaction, because the weakening of empire in Asia — and to some extent in

Africa — was causing "confusion, disintegration and dissolution" in Western Europe. What has already fallen or is still falling in 1949 is the system of empire in Asia; and what is baffling American policy is the fact that Marshall Plan blood transfusions to Western Europe are bleeding away from the wounds of colonial warfare in Asia.

To recover our balance, we must abandon the fantastic theory of "concentration of forces" which attempts to deal alternatingly with Europe and Asia. We must deal with the continuing interaction between them, which is a fact, not a theory. And we must not make the mistake of thinking that when we have defined a state or a people as "independent," "dependent," "subject," or "satellite," we have made our definitions precise enough. We must realize that both in Europe and in Asia the society within every state with which we deal is going through important changes. As the society within the state becomes a different kind of society, the state itself becomes a different kind of state. We can influence most of these changes. Not one of them can we stop. We must match the Russians in the realism with which we analyze what is happening in each process of change, and we must chasten the feeling of unlimited power with which we came out of the war. There are limits to our power. When power is limited, successful policy consists in doing what you can do in each situation, not in trying to do exactly what you would like to do, when you do not have what it takes.

For the average American, the briefest summary of

the outcome of the Second World War is that Germany and Japan were defeated. The average man in Asia cannot sum up the war so tersely. For him, some of the things that happened in the course of the war were as important as its final outcome. The fact that Japan, before being defeated, destroyed the old international balance of power and the structure of European imperial control throughout the Far East is as important for him as the fact that Japan was finally defeated.

For the peoples of colonial Asia, therefore, the end of the war meant that a supreme effort had yet to be made: an effort to set up quickly political structures that would take the place of the imperial control that Japan had destroyed, and prevent the return of their imperial rulers. For the people of China, there was a different but comparable challenge. Most of the "unequal treaties" had been abrogated before the end of the war, and the rest were abrogated soon after; but representative government had still to be won. The Kuomintang had been ruling them under the system which it called "tutelage," under which the Party appointed both national and local officials. Theoretically, the people were to be trained for representative self-government during the "period of tutelage"; but in fact the dictatorship of the Kuomintang had hardened. Had all Chinese waited meekly while the Kuomintang took back the territories held by the Japanese during the war, the dictatorship would have been in a condition to continue indefinitely. It was for this reason that American support of the Kuomintang government, purely on the grounds of "legitimacy," and without reference to the internal demand for the right to elect representatives to replace appointed Kuomintang officials, encouraged the suspicion of an indirect American control associated with the dictatorship of the Kuomintang. It was also for this reason that the Chinese Communists entered postwar politics as supporters of widely popular demands for regional rights and self-government through elected representatives.

In seizing the end of the war as an opportunity to prevent the return of old forms of government or the continuance of old forms of domination, the peoples of Asia resembled the peoples of Eastern Europe and the Balkans, whose primary concerns were to prevent both the restoration of Germany's imperial ascendancy over them and the transfer to other hands of Germany's old power to treat them politically and economically as a colonial domain. In this respect both Asia and Eastern Europe differed from Western Europe, where governments and voting majorities of citizens saw in the end of the war not opportunities but problems — problems in retaining or restoring as much as they could of their former advantages as the rulers of great empires.

In both Asia and Eastern Europe action was impossible — especially the swift action that alone could be effective — unless the motives for action were a mixture of nationalism and revolution. The proportions of the mixture differed between Eastern Europe and Asia, and between different countries in each region. The main difference was that there was more revolution in Eastern Europe and more nationalism in Asia. Unless the nature of this difference is clearly understood, very misleading analogies can be drawn between the Russian and Communist influences in the two regions.

In Eastern Europe, the victory over the Germans was won mainly by the Russians, and could not have been won without the Russians. Some of the Eastern European governments had been on the side of the Germans. Every one of them, with the exception of the government of Czechoslovakia, had been fascist or semi-fascist. In every single country, including Czechoslovakia, there had been important people — mostly factory owners, businessmen, and the larger landholders — who had collaborated with the Germans.

Nationalism, in such countries, meant getting rid of such people. To get rid of the menace which they embodied it was not enough to execute the most prominent individuals, or imprison them, or bar them from public office. They were a menace because they and the part of the society of Eastern Europe that they represented were built into the long-existing structure of the "colonial" relationship between Eastern Europe and Germany — a Germany which had been even more imperialistic under Hitler than it had been under the Hohenzollerns. Their forms of property and their economic functions within their own societies were part of the colonial mechanism by which Germany extracted raw materials from Eastern Europe, organized cartels to control the markets for factory-produced goods, and kept local industries and bankers subordinate to the industries and bankers of Germany.

This problem generated a friction within the societies of Eastern Europe which in turn generated the
fire of revolution. If collaborating individuals were
punished, but their property and the economic functions that went with the property were left in the
possession of their families and the social groups which
they represented, then the next generation would produce individuals with the same economic motivations
and political leanings. It was for this reason that socialists as well as Communists, and militant nationalists who
were neither socialists nor Communists, were in favor
of going beyond the punishment of individuals and
confiscating all forms of property that, in economic
function, had been useful in subordinating their countries to Germany.

With the inevitableness of a Greek tragedy, in
which both the players and the spectators know what
is going on but nobody can stop it, the doom of the
propertied classes in Eastern Europe poisoned all attempts to reach a cordial political understanding between the Western democracies and the "new democracies." In Western Europe, reconstruction meant just
that — the reconstruction of as much as possible of
what Germany had damaged or destroyed. In Eastern
Europe reconstruction meant the building of a new
structure, eliminating everything that had served subordination to Germany — and, in the larger sense, the
colonial inferiority of Eastern Europe to Western
Europe. Inexorably, this difference between restoring
as much as possible of what had existed before and re-

fusing to restore a key relationship that had existed before drove Western Europe into an increasingly dependent alliance with America and Eastern Europe into an increasingly dependent alliance with Soviet Russia.

We distort this picture of what really happened when we let ourselves be influenced too much either by the Russian and pro-Russian account of how "American imperialism" is reaching out to dominate Western Europe or by the anti-Russian account of how "Russian imperialism" has "annexed" Eastern Europe. There has been an expansion of American power; but there has also been Western Europe's own retreat into the arms of America. There has been an expansion of Russian power; but there has also been Eastern Europe's own retreat into the arms of Russia. (The striking exception, Yugoslavia's refusal to join this retreat, will be discussed in the next chapter.)

The relationship between Asia and Europe helps to explain how politics works in Western Europe. Though Western Europe shared in the defeat of Germany, it did not succeed — as it had after the First World War, under the Versailles treaties and the Danube Convention of 1921 — in staking out a claim to a share of Germany's imperial overlordship in Eastern Europe. In Asia, on the other hand, Western Europe retains footholds; and though they are only footholds, they are immensely valuable. In addition, Western Europe still holds colonial possessions in Africa that are many times greater than Europe itself.

Because of Asia and Africa the countries of Western

Europe, though they are democratic in their internal
structure, are imperial in their over-all structure. The
imperial ownership of one people by another is a direct
negation of democracy; and Western Europe's un-
democratic imperial relationship to its subject peoples
affects even the way in which democracy works at
home. The survival of empire is what explains the
strength of right-wing socialism and trade-unionism in
Britain, France, Holland, and Belgium. Empires exist
only because the owning country and people make a
profit out of the peoples that are owned. Full employment and good wages in an imperial country depend on the profits taken out of colonies. In an imperial
country even the labor movement and political parties
that depend on labor votes want to negotiate the independence of colonial peoples on terms that guarantee
them an economic compensation, and a gradual transition that eases the adjustment of changes in industry
and employment. Because they want this kind of protection for themselves, the right-wing socialists and
trade-unionists of Western Europe are willing to vote
for the principle of compensating the owners of nationalized industries. In this way the "bourgeois" and "proletarian" votes of Western Europe combine to support
the principle that postwar reconstruction should begin
by restoring, in the main, the structure and the system
that existed before Hitler, and should move only
slowly and cautiously toward the substitution of anything new.

In Asia there is no cleavage that corresponds to the
cleavage between Eastern and Western Europe. Asia

cannot be divided, like Europe, into countries that have their own colonial subjects and countries that do not. All countries in Asia except Turkey in the 1920's are, or recently have been, either the subjects of a foreign power or, like China and Siam, so dominated by foreign interests that their status was semi-colonial or quasi-colonial. Even Japan, once the most ruthless of all empires, is now an occupied country and economically lives on an American dole because it has been deprived of its colonial possessions.

It is true that every nation in Asia, except Korea, Japan, and Mongolia, has important internal minority problems. The biggest and most important problems of this kind are in China and India. China has to solve problems of internal imperialism in its relations with the Mongols of Inner Mongolia, the Chinese Moslems, the Uighurs and other peoples of Sinkiang, the Tibetans, and the tribes of Southwest China. But the nationalism of these peoples wants exactly what the nationalism of China itself wants, and therefore the problem can be solved by granting autonomy to the minorities, followed by federalization on an equality with the Chinese.

Throughout Asia, therefore, the primary phenomenon is nationalism — the demand for complete independence. The achievement of independence is inevitably accompanied by some degree of social transformation in each country; but this revolutionary transformation is not so drastic as in Europe.

The subservience of the Czech or Hungarian banker to German bankers, and sometimes to French

or British bankers, was all too often a willing subservience. He made bigger profits by such associations
than if he attempted to remain independent. All too
often, if the preservation of this kind of interest demanded that he work politically for the subordination
of his country, he was willing to do so. The Chinese or
Indian banker was also subservient to foreign bankers;
but not willingly. Modern banking in these countries
began with the foreigner. Britain ruled India, and
European and American bankers in China were so
completely beyond the control of the Chinese government that they were able to issue their own paper currency. Foreign bankers in China paid no taxes, and
their influence over the Chinese government was so
great that it could be said that instead of suffering from
taxation without representation, they had the astonish-
ing privilege of representation without taxation. Chinese and Indian bankers had to fight their way into the
market in their own countries. They could increase
their profits better by winning full independence than
by remaining subservient. Since they could win full
independence as bankers only if their country won
true independence as a nation, they financed nationalist
movements and made alliances even with left-wingers.

In Asia, in the social transformation that accom-
panies the achievement of national independence, the
bitterest struggle has not been between capitalists and
the proletariat but between feudal landholders and the
peasantry. A word of explanation is needed here. The
word "feudal" is used so loosely that it causes a great
deal of unnecessary confusion. Particularly as Marx-

ists use it, it has tended to become a general term of abuse instead of a precise term of description.

Feudal land tenure in Asia is a noncapitalistic way of owning and using land. In a progressive and creative capitalism, capital works. It makes things. It also grows crops, on farms, in ways that would not be possible without the investment of capital. In typical, capitalistic American farming the capital that goes into machinery, fertilizers, seed selection, and every step that improves farming is as important as the capital that goes into the purchase of land. In the typical farming of Asia, possession of the land is what counts. The landlord uses his possession of the land simply to force peasants to bid against each other for the opportunity to cultivate it. If a tenant has been delivering 60 per cent of the crop to the landlord he can be evicted if another peasant offers to deliver 70 per cent. There are, of course, many variations of this theme. There are millions of peasant families in Asia that own a little bit of land — often in several tiny pieces, two or three miles from each other — but not enough to live on, so that they have to rent additional land from a landlord, as share croppers. If such a family falls behind on its deliveries, it may have to mortgage its own land to the landlord. Frequently the landlord forecloses on this mortgage; which means that he adds to his holding of land without paying a cent for it in cash.

A feudal society splits up in rivalries among the privileged landholders unless there is an overlord strong enough both to regulate these rivalries and to

enforce the right of the individual landholder to collect his tribute from the peasant. This overlordship
was formerly provided by the old despotic empires of
Asia itself. In ruling their subjects in Asia, the European empires took over this function. The peasant
became the subject both of his landholder and of the
foreign ruler; the landholder was the subject of the
foreign ruler in some respects, but his ally in others.
He was loyal to the foreign ruler to the exact degree
that the form of rule protected his kind of property;
and since his kind of property was the last that the
foreign ruler ceased to be able to protect, he remained
loyal to imperialist rule long after other groups in
colonial societies had turned nationalist.

Peasants respond to the same law of self-interest.
Throughout Asia, peasants become loyal to nationalist
parties, and later on to nationalist governments, in proportion to the willingness of the nationalists to loosen
the landlord's grip on them. To the extent that the
new government favors and protects the kind of
ownership of land that they want, they consider it
"their" government and support it. The identification
between loyalty to the government and devotion to
one's own kind of property is a political law that is
valid even in Soviet Russia. Divided loyalties weakened Russia most in the terrible and bloody struggle
over collectivization, a thinly disguised civil war in
which land was taken from the rich peasants and given
to poor peasants, not individually but as members of
collective farms. Since then, a new kind of loyalty has
gradually solidified as more and more Soviet peasants

in the Ukraine, Russia, Siberia, and Soviet Asia have come to feel that their individual shares in collective farms represent a kind of ownership more valuable to them than the old private ownership under which they were unable to own or even hire machines.

In the general pattern of society in Asia, the proportion of peasants varies a little from country to country, but the average is about 80 per cent. The modern middle class, which has grown up under Western rule or Western influence, is small in numbers. Though both this middle class and the landlords are property-minded, there is no inevitable political alliance between them, because they own different kinds of property and use their property in different ways. The landlord has a pre-modern mind. He thinks of his land as conferring a privilege on him; he uses this privilege to collect tribute from his tenant. The man of the modern middle class — banker, industrialist, professional man, white collar worker — has a modern, cost-accounting mind. He thinks of investment and interest, salaries and savings, and money rather than land as the unit of wealth in much the same way as the same kind of man in Western countries. Unlike the landlord, he does not willingly accept a foreign ruler; because the foreign ruler, who keeps the landlord in business, keeps the colonial banker and industrialist either out of business or in the lower, less profitable ranks of business.

Politics in Asia is an equation in which there is one constant, and a number of variables. The constant factor is the antagonism of the peasant to the landlord. Because he fears the demands of the peasants, the landlord is the last to give up his loyalty to a foreign ruler who is no longer able to rule, and the first to make terms — as in Indonesia now — with a foreign ruler who looks as though he might be on his way back to power. The middle class, with its interest in capitalism, is the most changeable. It can be either extremely conservative or astonishingly radical. Before liberation, it will ally itself with radical movements against imperialism. After liberation, it may ally itself with the landlords, in an alliance of the haves against the have-nots, or it may put up a fight against the landlords for the control of the country as a whole.

In India under British rule the princes of the Native States, whose power was of a feudal kind, were both the subjects and the allies of the British. In the Union of India, whose government is controlled by an alliance between Nehru, a socialist, and Patel, the organizer of the business interests, the most important privileges of the princes were promptly taken away by a combination of negotiation and pressure; armed action was needed to bring under control Hyderabad, the greatest of the principalities.

In China, there have been combinations and recombinations. Twenty-five years ago, the main drive of nationalism was against the Unequal Treaties, which protected the rights and privileges won by a number of foreign nations in the great age of imperialism in the second half of the nineteenth century. Chinese bankers and industrialists, unable to compete effectively in their own country against treaty-protected foreigners, suffered more from the effects of the treaties than did the landlords. Among the followers

of Sun Yat-sen, it was they who agreed to bring the
peasants and industrial workers into the Kuomintang,
even though it meant working with the Chinese Communists, Russian advisors, and a number of other
foreign Communists sent by the Third International.

When, after the death of Sun Yat-sen, the nationalist *élan* of the peasant armies carried the Kuomintang to the Yangtze and Shanghai, the great powers,
led by Britain, were ready to negotiate a deal with
Chinese nationalism rather than risk the immediate
loss of all their privileges. The deal involved smashing
the political organizations of the peasants and the industrial workers, and therefore an alliance between the
landlords and the bankers and industrialists. The key
figure in the deal was Chiang Kai-shek, because he had
at one time been a businessman and broker in Shanghai
and had business contacts in Shanghai, Canton, and
among the wealthy overseas Chinese in Malaya, while
his contacts in the army were with officers who came
from landlord families.

In the 1930's, Japan was encroaching on China.
Chiang Kai-shek continued his civil war against the
Communists, claiming that until he had completely
destroyed them China would be in no condition to
face Japan. The capitalists of China grew increasingly
uneasy. Their interests were on the coast, and suffered from Japan's increasing control of trade. They
responded, to a degree that would surprise American
capitalists, to the Communist demand for a cessation
of civil war and a united front against Japan. The
landlords, on the other hand, feared the peasants more
than Japan and insisted on continuing the civil war.

The fact that Chiang continued the civil war showed that even then his position was more dependent on landlord than on capitalist support. In addition he calculated — quite correctly, and more accurately than American experts — that Japan's continuing aggression would bring on war with America; though the war did not come as soon as he hoped, and of course America's inability to crush Japan at once, after the Pearl Harbor disaster, was an unforeseen and dismaying disappointment.

War between China and Japan was finally forced by the spontaneous resistance of rank-and-file Chinese troops in North China. The resistance was so extensive, and the outburst of nationalist fervor that responded to it so overwhelming, that the government was carried along.

As soon as Shanghai, Hankow, and Canton were lost the most important Chinese capitalists lost the sources of their wealth and therefore their political power. The "free China" of the Kuomintang was dominated by landlord interests, which dictated a "standstill" war, waiting for America to defeat Japan and for American support against the Communists. Guerrilla China was dominated by Communist-led peasants. The need for keeping their leadership dictated for the Communists an active war and the steady organization of the kind of landownership and village self-government demanded by the peasants.

The end of the war showed the complete ascendancy of the landlords in the Kuomintang. Business and industry in great cities like Shanghai, instead of being returned to private capitalists, were placed under government monopolies. The Chinese Communist term for this system is "bureaucratic monopoly," which is somewhat misleading. It is essentially an attempt to bring modern economic activities under feudal control. The feudal mind, instead of thinking in terms of cost accounting and rational management, wants the kind of privilege that gives the right to collect tribute, regardless of cost and not in return for services rendered. A textile industry, to take an example of a monopoly under feudal control, is not regarded as a rational operation. It is a position of advantage in which to place sons, nephews, and in-laws. If they can make money faster by selling cotton on the black market than by weaving it into cloth, supplying the consumer market, lowering prices, and stabilizing economic conditions, that is regarded as businesslike enough.

One of the grand American delusions has been the idea that supporting people who have this feudal conception of the nature of property and the rights of the individual is somehow the same thing as "supporting capitalism." We fumble in such things partly because we have had practically no experience of feudalism in the United States; but everywhere in Europe, where capitalism replaced feudalism, it did so by confiscating feudal property and turning it into capitalist property. Thereafter, the capitalists survived or failed individually, according to their ability to think in cost-accounting values and to make money out of either goods supplied or services rendered.

In China, the American inability to distinguish between feudalism and capitalism drove Chinese capitalists, managers, and technicians frantic. American policy, not Communist propaganda, convinced them first that they could not do business with Chiang and finally that they could perhaps do business with the Communists. In the final debacle, they began to go over to the Communists, in exactly the manner called for by the Stalin prescription already quoted: "when the so-called neutral elements, all that mass of many millions of city and village petty bourgeoisie, begin definitely to turn away from the adversary . . . and seeks alliance with the proletariat." The American improvement on the prescription was to add a good many really big and important capitalists to the "petty bourgeoisie."

We are learning that there are societies within which we cannot stop the processes of change. If we admit that we cannot stop change, can we discover ways in which we can influence change so that it will be more in our favor? We are learning that there are limits to our power. If we admit that, then where is there a line that is within the limits of our power to which we can withdraw and from which we can operate effectively?

The first step toward finding an answer to these questions is to find the line marking the limit of Russian power. When we have found that line, we shall find that there is a big geographical gap, including most of Asia, between the limit of our power and the limit of Russian power. We shall then find that the problem of policy is how to deal best from our side with this area that is out of control, while the Russians deal with it as best they can from their side.

CHAPTER V

RUSSIA'S FRONTIER IN ASIA

IN THE affairs of Asia, the United States is on the outside, looking in. The great imperial countries of
Europe are on the doorstep, trying not to be pushed
off. Russia is on the inside, looking out. Russia has not
only a land frontier of actual contact with Asia, but a
frontier running through Asia. From Korea on the
Yellow Sea to Turkey on the Black Sea, it is the longest
frontier in the world. Many sectors of it are not held
by Russians on one side, facing various peoples of Asia
on the other, but by Asians who form part of the
federal Soviet state facing Asians who live under
various kinds of governments, many of them hostile
to the Soviet system.

On most sectors of the frontier the line separates
politically peoples who, in spite of differences in the
form of government, are really one and the same
people in language, historical tradition, and other cultural characteristics. The same languages and dialects
are spoken on both sides of the Soviet-Turkish frontier. Soviet Azerbaijan fronts on Iranian Azerbaijan.
The Soviet-Afghan frontier separates similar peoples.
The Kirghiz and Kazakhs of Soviet territory are ex-

actly the same peoples as the Kirghiz and Kazakhs of Chinese Sinkiang. The Soviet Buryat-Mongols have a common frontier with the Outer Mongolian People's Republic.

The Soviet frontier in Asia therefore has a peculiar political sensitiveness. When a people who are one people are divided by a political frontier, loyalties conflict. The two governments may be hostile to each other while most of the people on both sides of the line are friendly to each other. In such cases, each of the two governments always has to deal with the fact that some of the people on its side of the line would prefer to live under the government on the other side of the line, or to make their own government like the government on the other side. One of the two governments may be bothered by only a small number of discontented or dissident people, while for the other the problem is of major importance. It is easy to exploit such a situation by propaganda. What each government has to say about the other, however, is not what creates the situation. Basically, the situation is created by what each government does to or for its own people.

Iranian Azerbaijan illustrates how this relationship works. During the war, Russia occupied the north of Iran while Britain occupied the south. After the war, Russia refused to withdraw. (The British withdrew, but kept their political influence alive by paying subsidies to tribal chieftains in South Iran.) In 1946 the Russians withdrew, under strong United Nations pressure led by the United States; but an "autonomous"

regime in Iranian Azerbaijan, where the majority of
the population are not Iranians, continued to prevent
the Iranian government from exercising full authority.
The autonomous regime had the aid of organizers
from Soviet Azerbaijan. It began some reforms, the
most important of which strengthened peasants against
landlords. Many landlords left the province. Peasants
liked the reforms but were cautious in supporting the
autonomous government, waiting to see whether the
landlords would come back.

In 1947 the landlords came back. The Iranian government had been strengthened by American aid, and
American policy encouraged it to assert its rights over
Azerbaijan. The tough work in taking back the province was not done by regular troops but by bands
recruited by the returning landlords. Resistance was
light, and was not whipped up by Soviet propaganda.

Iranian Azerbaijan has thus seen something of two
kinds of reality, which is more important than the two
kinds of propaganda to which it has also been sub-
jected. The reforms of the autonomous period were
imitative of Soviet Azerbaijan, though there was no
full revolution leading to sovietization and collectivization. The landlords, when they returned, took reprisals
on all whom they could catch who had been associated
with the reforms. There was more killing and violence
in undoing the reforms than there had been in putting
them into effect in the first place. Unfortunately, in
backward countries where the rights of the individual
are not respected unless he is rich and powerful, this
is always true. The Iranian government is as corrupt

and inefficient as it ever was. The numbers of the poor, the discontented, and the underfed are as great as they have always been. The police, however, with American equipment and training under American advisors, are more efficient than they were before, and the rich and powerful are better protected.

The Azerbaijanians will read this lesson in politics in only one way: "It is frightening to have the Russians come in and upset the old ways of life and start reforms of which we do not know the final outcome; but it is worse to have the Iranians come back. If we drive the Iranians out again, we had better be rough enough to make it stick. As for landlords, it is better to kill them than to let them get away and come back with their armed gangs." The lesson is more than academic. There will be another rising in Azerbaijan — perhaps before the end of 1949. It will be aided by the Russians and encouraged by Russian propaganda; but it will not be the political creation of the Russians. It will spring from the nature of the relationship between the people of Iranian Azerbaijan and the government at Teheran.

When the Russian Revolution broke out most of Russia's neighbors in Asia were not anxious to join in, except for the Mongols of Outer Mongolia, who had been given such a rough going-over first by Chinese militarists and then by antirevolutionary Russians that their nationalism, already militant, took a revolutionary turn. In the first years after the revolution, the new and terrifying thing called Bolshevism was more feared than admired in countries along the edge of

Russia. In Asia, prosperous Turkmenians, Uzbeks, Kazakhs, and Buryats, as well as Russians, escaped into adjoining territories. The tales that they carried with them were tales of terror. There was no news of any reforms of a kind that brought comfort or ease of living.

Then, especially after the Five-Year Plans began, there were changes. There were more schools and hospitals. There were improvements in the techniques of agriculture. Industries began to develop. More and more people had opportunities to learn and do things which for them were more interesting than their old ways of life. Of course in such countries on the European edge of Russia as Finland and the Baltic states only small minorities were attracted by the news of improvements in Russia. These improvements had not caught up with what they themselves already had. In such countries there was a comfortable, middle-class standard of life, with good opportunities for education. In Finland, at least, even the peasants were still for the most part better off than most of the peasants in Russia.

In Asia, the improvements and new opportunities in the Asian republics of the Soviet Union loomed much bigger. Along the entire length of the frontier in Asia, the new Soviet order was in touch with peoples who had never known such a thing as even a modestly prosperous European middle-class way of living. A few rich people lived in a barbaric kind of luxury; they had plenty of servants and plenty to eat, but few mechanical conveniences. Very few, even among the rich, had good medical attention. Many of them were ignorant and only half-literate; and even the rich knew that their own countries were practically helpless in dealing with Great Britain, the great power of the Middle East, or the European rulers of the colonial countries, or Japan, the great power of the Far East. They knew that when foreigners came into their countries to develop oil, or to open banks, or to engage in large-scale trade, the big profits went to the foreigners and only small pickings to the native hangers-on of the foreigners.

The poor, in these countries along the edge of Russia, were pitifully poor. Their houses, their clothes, their food were all miserable. Infant mortality was appalling. A woman was old and worn-out before she was thirty. Only a few of the poor ever went to school; and if they did, they learned almost nothing of practical value. There was electricity in only a few large cities. Nobody farmed with tractors. Their rents were excessive, their taxes high, and out of their taxes they got back nothing in the way of public services. In practically every country in Asia, the soldier and the policeman were not looked to as protectors, but dreaded as people whose coming always meant something bad for the poor and helpless.

Among Russia's neighbors in Asia, the progress made in the Soviet republics of Asia from about 1925 to 1941 inspired awe and wonder. The virtual civil war of the collectivization drive and the harshness of the political purges did not shock them as they shocked Russia's neighbors in Europe. Throughout Asia, it

was taken as a matter of course that those in power
should, from time to time, make a display of their
power and rattle the teeth of anybody who might
seem to defy them in even a mild and indirect way. It
never even entered their heads to ask questions about
political democracy in connection with what they
heard about events in Russia. In their own countries,
there was no such thing, and the people in all countries
— even America — do not compare things that they
hear about with things that they have not heard about.

In those years, as I know myself from experience, if
the subject of American democracy were to crop up
in a conversation with some ordinary man living somewhere near the Russian frontier, about the most intelligent comment that you could expect would be that
"all Americans are rich, and therefore they all have
the same rights." I have also heard "democracy" used
as a novel word to describe something that the user
thought was a good idea. In 1937, on a steamer in the
Mediterranean, I ran into some pilgrims going to
Mecca. They were Uighurs from Sinkiang, who had
traveled overland through Russia and then across the
Black Sea to Turkey. In Russia they had been hand-
somely treated, for propaganda purposes of course. I
asked them what money they used, traveling through
so many countries. They showed me little bags of gold
dust. I said that I thought that the Russians confiscated
all gold, giving paper rubles instead. "Oh, no," they
said, "haven't you heard? The Russians have democracy. They are good to Moslems."

Minorities, of course, continued to be afraid of even

a "progressive" Russia. A rich man with a lot of property, living in a weak country, is made nervous by the news that the country next door to him, after taking away the property of the rich, has become even more powerful than it was when it was ruled by rich men. Growing majorities, however, were impressed by tales of the Soviet way of doing things. It leads to daydreams when a poor peasant lad in Iranian Azerbaijan, or a poor Kazakh shepherd in Sinkiang, hears that in Soviet Azerbaijan or Soviet Kazakhstan a poor boy from a family exactly like his, speaking exactly the same language, can go to school with all expenses paid by the state, and on through school to the university, to become an engineer, or a doctor, or a high official, or anything that he is good enough to be. He thinks it wonderful that in those countries his position could be as good as that of a Russian, and that if his position were high he would have Russians under him, because in Russia those things, at least in theory, depend on a man's ability, not on his race.

The idea that a man from a minority can be equal, as an individual, to a man from a majority is a novel idea, because throughout Asia minorities are oppressed. If a traveler from America, passing through, were to tell such a boy that his opportunities in America would be just as good, he would be glad to hear it; but for him, going to America is a fantastic idea, while going to Russia is excitingly close to being a practical idea.

During and since the war there have been setbacks to the reputation that Russia had earned in Asia by the propaganda of things done, as compared with the propaganda of things said. The war itself was a terrible ordeal. The rate of casualties in the mechanized war with the Germans was beyond anything in the experience of Asia. The Soviet peoples of Asia were still near enough to their experience under the Tsars to be ready to suspect very easily that the Russians used them as cannon fodder to save Russian casualties. (In much the same way it became a saying, among the Indian troops used by the British in Italy, that "we are put in the front line to storm the city, but the British march at the head of the column when we parade through the city.") German propaganda helped to work up distrust between non-Russians and Russians. German linguists were good, and they spread through leaflets and pamphlets a propaganda that was technically much more skillful than that used, for example, by the Japanese against the Chinese Communists.

The Russians had trouble during the war with some of the Tatars of South Russia, the Kalmuk Mongols of the lower Volga, and some of the tribes in the Caucasus. On the whole, however, they came out of this ordeal well, as compared with any nation using "minority" troops during the war. The Kazakhs, whom the Tsarist Russians had never dared to use as troops, sent entire cavalry divisions into the war, under Kazakh command. Numbers of these Kazakhs, after being captured by the Germans and liberated by the Americans or British, have said that they do not want to go back. On the other hand there seems to have been no political trouble in the huge land of Kazakhstan during the war, whereas during the First World

War there were serious risings against Tsarist Russia.

During the war, the Russians deliberately roused their own Russian patriotism, and with it Russian nationalism, to reinforce Soviet patriotism. Since the war, this strident Russian nationalism may have grated on the competitive nationalism of the smaller, non-Russian peoples within the Soviet Union. It certainly has stirred misgivings in Soviet satellite countries and other countries bordering on the Soviet Union. Old fears of "Russification" have revived.

In the last weeks of the war against Japan, when the Russians came in at the kill, their Outer Mongolian allies contributed two columns or armies of Russian-equipped, Russian-trained, but Mongol-commanded troops. These columns cut through Inner Mongolia on their way into Manchuria. There was cordial fraternization. The Mongols of Outer Mongolia had for twenty years been under a revolutionary government of their own, independent in fact though not internationally recognized, and under strong Russian influence. During this period Inner Mongolia had remained at first under Chinese rule, under which the Mongols suffered steady encroachment and loss of their land by Chinese colonization. Later, most of Inner Mongolia had come under Japanese control. The Japanese encouraged the Mongols to act independently toward the Chinese, but divided the part of Inner Mongolia they occupied into two "protectorates," in which they supported a nonrevolutionary nationalism headed by the hereditary princes and the high ecclesiastical authorities of Lama-Buddhism.

The Mongols took it for granted after the war that all Mongol-inhabited territory would henceforth be united in one "Greater Mongolia." Even hereditary princes visited Ulan Bator, capital of revolutionary Outer Mongolia, and were cordially received. Then suddenly Outer Mongolia cooled and hardened in its attitude toward Inner Mongolia. The border was closed. Nationalists of Inner Mongolia interpreted this to mean that Russia, in fear of international complications, had forbidden Outer Mongolia to go ahead with Mongol unification. This in turn they interpreted to mean that though Outer Mongolia — the Mongolian People's Republic — is nominally independent and an "equal" ally of Russia, its interests are actually subordinated and sacrificed to the "high policy" of Russia.

In Europe, as in Asia, there is the same feeling among those whom the Russians call allies, and whom we call the satellites of Russia, that when the going is tough their interests are sacrificed to the overriding interests of Russia. Such apprehensions are heightened by war scares. It is a dogma with the Russians, or something perilously close to a dogma, that eventually America is going to lead the capitalist world in a "preventive" war against them. When a war scare makes it look as though theory might materialize into fact, the Russians feel constrained to consolidate their defenses, and to do so by tightening up the centralization of all controls in their own home territory, which they consider the heart of the socialist world of the future.

When under the pressure of a war scare, the Russians feel that there is no time to take it easy, to explain and persuade, or to ease transitional processes from capitalism to socialism in countries like Yugoslavia, Czechoslovakia, Poland, or Outer Mongolia. They sacrifice the "federalizing" aspect of nominal political voting equality between big and little states in the Cominform to what they think is the compelling need for harsh military centralization.

The story of Titoism throws light on this side of Russian policy. The Hoover Report on reorganization of the executive branch of the government revealed that in the spring of 1948 there was an acute war scare in Washington, based on a mistaken intelligence report from the Air Force. We prepared to go on a war footing. Within weeks, the Tito crisis between Yugoslavia and the Cominform broke into the open. Only one inference is possible. The Russians knew of the war scare in Washington, and reacted to it as a threat that they would be attacked. They tightened up their own controls. Sessions of the Cominform became less like consultations between countries with kindred interests and more like general staff sessions in which the Russians gave the orders and the subordinate countries were expected to carry them out. Tito, feeling that the sacrifices demanded of Yugoslavia were disproportionate, broke away. There were repercussions in Czechoslovakia and Poland, but these countries were held in line.

Presumably, when the Russians tighten up in an emergency, they get at least the minimum results that they consider necessary. But these results are subject to their own law of diminishing returns: control is increased, within the geographical range in which control is possible; but beyond the line where Russian policy must begin to operate through influence instead of control, Russian influence diminishes. The fact that Russia is subject to this law of diminishing returns proves again that although the Soviet Union is the only country that approaches the United States in the magnitude of its power, Russian power, like American power, has its limits. The limits of power are different for the two countries, but they work in the same way. To the extent that America tightens up control over Western Europe, forbidding Marshall Plan countries to trade in certain categories of goods with Eastern Europe, because this trade, though it would benefit them, would also benefit Russia, we infringe on their sovereignty. We appear to justify the Russian propaganda, by reducing them from the status of allies to the status of satellites. We tighten up control, where we are able to exercise control, but we lose influence in areas where, not having control, our policy is forced to depend on influence.

These comparisons show that both in Asia and in Europe politics work through a double process. There is a politics of attraction and a politics of repulsion. Both processes are evident along the geographical limits of the power of the European empires in Asia, and the limits of American and Russian power. When countries in Asia appear to be gravitating toward Russia, it may be either because they are attracted by what Russia itself is doing, or because they are repelled by

the policies of the European powers or America.
When they appear to be recoiling from Russia, it
may be because of what Russia is doing, or it may
be because they are attracted by the policy of America or one of the European countries. Frequently,
both processes are at work at the same time.

It is quite understandable that there should be times
when countries close to Russia are repelled, while distant countries are attracted. At the time of the Russian
Revolution, Russia's weak neighbors in Asia were re-
lieved that such a powerful empire had fallen; but the
bloodshed and disorder of the revolution frightened
them and sharply checked any impulse to join in.
More distant people saw the advantages more clearly
and were less affected by the feeling of danger. The
mere existence of a revolutionary Russia was a great
encouragement to the colonial unrest in Asia after the
First World War. Sun Yat-sen at Canton, far in the
south of China, was repelled by the coldness toward
him of the British and American officials whom he
tried to approach, and eagerly welcomed the chance
to co-operate with Russia.

The Russians can damage their own power to attract peoples who look to them for sympathy. In
1946 they decided that, all things considered, they had
better pull their troops out of Manchuria. They were
not sure that America would respond to this gesture —
and in fact the American Marines were not withdrawn
from China until a good deal later, and American
planes and ships were active in transporting the troops
of Chiang Kai-shek — so they played it safe. Advance

agents of the Chinese Communists were already in Manchuria, eager to take over the great industries built up by the Japanese. They were sure they could swing it. The Russians were not so sure. They were afraid that Manchuria, if its industries were left a going concern, might be turned into an American stronghold on the doorstep of Siberia, so they gutted the factories of Manchuria as they withdrew. The Chinese Communists, confident of their own abilities and loyal to Russia in all questions of common world policy, found this very hard to take. It was a ruthless example of the sacrifice of the interests of non-Russian Communists to the paramount interest of the Soviet Union.

On the whole, however, the Russian power of attraction in Asia has not diminished, at least potentially. It owes a great deal to the way in which European and American policies have repelled so many countries and peoples. Colonial peoples, attacked by their former rulers and shot down by American guns, increasingly feel that Russia is their only friend. India and Pakistan, though anti-Communist, like to be treated by Russia as countries which have genuine interests of their own, not subordinate to an overriding British or American interest. Neither of these countries can be converted into a willing ally against Russia, because to turn against Russia would in fact subordinate them to an overriding Anglo-American interest. Israel, though its political philosophy is closer to that of the British Labour Government than to that of any other government in the world, is repelled by the morose anti-Semitism of Foreign Secretary Ernest Bevin and by the British policy of supporting Arab princes who represent arbitrary privilege, subjection of the people to a hereditary aristocracy, and every form of social abuse that, in Britain itself, the Labour Government is pledged to abolish. This repulsion acts very much in the same way as if Israel were drawn toward Russia by attraction.

Elsewhere in the Near East nationalism will inevitably turn against the present rulers, whose highest idea of statesmanship is to sell the oil resources of their countries to British and American concessionaires, in return for royalties which they treat as personal income, not as state revenues for the benefit of the people. In proportion as this form of nationalism develops, the repulsion of Anglo-American policy will increasingly make it appear as though a powerful force of attraction toward Russia were at work.

The strength and weakness of the Soviet position in Asia match each other. One major advantage held by the Soviet Union is that its frontiers, in both Europe and Asia, actually touch the frontier of only one country massive enough to be a future great world power. That country is China. All other countries whose frontiers touch the Soviet Union are not only weak, but are much below the Russian level in modern technology and industrialization. The only close neighbors of Russia that rank with Russia in technological quality are Czechoslovakia and possibly Finland; but these two countries are units too small to become independent centers of power. For all the

other countries that ring the Soviet frontiers, Russia
not only holds a central position but is the nearest
geographical center of modern civilization, technology, and industry. This fact, which is of enormous
importance, especially in Asia, is easily overlooked
from America, because from the American point of
view Russia technologically is a country lagging behind, not a country in advance.

The fact that Russia is strong, geographically holds
a central position, and is technologically far in advance
of the weak countries that surround it makes easy a
modern resumption of the old Tsarist "incorporative"
expansion. If Russia helps to develop an adjoining
country, that country not only acquires a more modern economy but tends to become incorporated with
the larger Russian mass. In this particular respect, it
may sometimes be a quibble to distinguish politically
between a country actually annexed by Russia, like
the former People's Republic of Tannu Tuva, and a
country like the Mongolian People's Republic, whose
government technically is allied with the Soviet
Union, not incorporated into it.

The Mongols themselves want certain things — machines, industrially produced goods, technicians. They
want these things for their own reasons, not because
they have somehow been hypnotized by Russian propaganda into wanting the good things of life. They can
get these things only from the Russians — partly because they are next door to Russia. America, the
only other country that could at present supply them,
voted against admitting the Mongolian People's Re-

public into the United Nations and has no diplomatic or trade relations with it. But the Russians are
themselves hard-pressed economically. They can afford to supply goods and lend technicians, even to a
good neighbor, only if the neighbor uses them in
ways which, in addition to benefiting itself, benefit
its common interests with Russia. In such a situation,
it is more or less a matter of convenience whether the
two countries co-ordinate their interests through alliances and trade pacts between the two governments
or through federalization.

The Russian kind of strength can be seen to its
best advantage in Korea, a country in which it is in
competition with the American kind of strength.
When Japan fell, the Korean passion for liberty
was at explosion point. There are about 25,000,000
Koreans. They are one of the few nations in Asia that
have no minority problems. There is virtually no non-
Korean population in the country since the Japanese
have been shipped out. There had been thirty-six
years of Japanese rule, marked by an especially brutal
police oppression. Even the Korean language had
been forbidden in Korean schools since 1937. Eighty
per cent of the wealth of the country had passed into
Japanese hands. All that the Koreans wanted was
liberation and a chance to form their own government.

What they got was a stern military government
under the Russians in the north and a military government under the Americans in the south which was not
equally stern, but was equally tight in its grip on
power. Gradually, as the Americans began to pass

power back to the Koreans, only one rule was applied: no power must get into the hands of Koreans who might work with the Russians. This limitation forced the Americans to work with two kinds of people: returned political exiles, and Koreans who had collaborated with the Japanese. The returned exiles had only a shaky popularity because, although their names were known and respected, they had no network of actual organization in the country. The scanty network that existed was the Korean underground, which was leftist. The collaborators were detested by the Koreans, but had a kind of dingy respectability in American eyes because they were supposed, through their affiliation with the Japanese, to know something about keeping the people under control; and the people were the main danger if a big swing toward the Russians were to develop.

We are safe in assuming that the Russians, also, were guided by a rule that power must not be put into the hands of Koreans who might turn to the Americans. This meant that the Russians had to rely on the factory workers and the beaten-down masses of the peasantry, which suited them in any case.

The deciding factor was the disposal of Japanese-owned property. When 80 per cent of the wealth of a country, including not only the factories but all the farming land worth owning, is in the hands of hated conquerors, and the conquerors are suddenly removed, the people who get their hands on most of the property formerly owned by the conquerors automatically become a ruling class. It is as simple as that. Most of the industrial property in Korea is in the north, which gave the Russians something of a proletariat with which to work. South Korea is mainly agricultural, which multiplied the problems of the Americans, whose Military Government had not the faintest comprehension of the kinds of animosity that are aroused in Asia by the struggle over land between peasants and landlords.

A "land reform" was attempted by the Americans, but was bound to be a farce. The peasants had no capital. The Koreans who had collaborated with the Japanese and the Koreans who had served in the Japanese police knew how to look after themselves when land was redistributed. They also knew all the tricks of how to get land away from peasants. Sooner or later they were bound to get most of the land into their possession, reducing the peasants to tenancy again. They knew this, and the peasants knew it. Only the Americans did not. The result has been the steady growth in South Korea, not of pro-Russian feeling but of the conviction that the former friends of the Japanese, now the friends of the Americans, must be driven out if South Korea is to get together with North Korea and form a nation.

The problem was thus simplified for the Russians. The Americans had set up for them exactly the conditions under which there would be the least effectual Korean resistance to a Russian-type land reform. To make sure that the land stayed with the peasants to whom it was given, the Russians had to do two things. They had to organize peasant unions, so that farm labor could be co-operatively organized, thus making up as far as possible for the deficiency of capital; and they had to deprive of power those Koreans who knew the legal and political tricks of getting peasants into debt and out of their land. The problem largely solved itself: Koreans of this kind made for the border as fast as they could, in order to join up with the similar Koreans who were already getting the key political and economic jobs with the Americans.

The factories were easy to nationalize. Because they had all belonged to the Japanese, no Koreans had to be expropriated. In addition, Korean industry had been developed as a subsidiary to Japanese industry. Cut off from Japan, it could not stand alone and had to be integrated with Russian industry in Siberia. The Russians had only to organize labor unions, import technicians, and begin to train a new Korean management under nationalized ownership.

The finishing touches climaxed the difference between Russian and American methods. The Russians organized a national army, grounding it on peasants who had land to defend and industrial workers who considered the new government their own, since it had been based on the protection of their rights. The army was equipped with Russian material, not captured Japanese material. The Russians were able to withdraw their occupation forces by the end of 1948. There is every reason to believe that they left behind them a North Korea in which a substantial number of people intensely dislike the new order of things; but there is also no reason to doubt that the army will fight, that the new government has enough grass-roots support to stay solidly in power, and that a new personnel of technicians and management is forming, probably rather rapidly, which looks to Russia as the source of all skill and wisdom.

In South Korea the Americans organized not a national army, but a constabulary, the backbone of which consists of men who served in the police under the Japanese — the most hated of all who collaborated with the Japanese. There has already been one serious mutiny in this force, and there will be more. Syngman Rhee, a returned exile, is at the head of the political structure. He has completely tainted himself by his wholehearted association with the relatively prosperous, crooked, and pliable Koreans who collaborated with the Japanese. Various enterprises have been "nationalized," but have been staffed with personnel in political favor, whose outlook is not one of serving the state but one of building individual power for themselves and eventually converting public property into private property. Land reform has resulted in a large increase in the number of owners of land, but control of the land, through the political, administrative, and tax machinery, is in the hands of politicians whose idea of farming is to be a landlord, not a working proprietor. Peasant dissatisfaction has already been shown in a number of risings; there will be more.

The army cannot be trusted to fight; the people do not trust the government; the government cannot be depended on, and does not depend on itself: it appeals for continued American occupation and protection. If there is to be a civil war, South Korea would not be able to subdue North Korea without a great deal more American help than is now available. North Korea would be able to overrun South Korea without Russian help, unless stopped by American combat troops. America, which has in China complained of the bad luck of having inherited the Kuomintang through no fault of its own, has in Korea manufactured its own Kuomintang. To support our proclaimed policy of world-wide opposition to police states, we have in South Korea created a weak and unreliable police state of our own.

The limitations of Russian power appear in countries like Iran and Afghanistan. These countries do not have large, Japanese-built industries, as Korea has, or a sufficient network of modern roads for rapid movement. Their revolutionary movements are not strong enough to start up on their own and then turn to the Russians for aid — though the separatist movement in Iranian Azerbaijan may become strong enough to do so within a year or two. The Russians do not have enough goods to spare to dominate the markets of these countries. Economically, they are still so hard-pressed that they must trade where they can get things that they really need themselves. Nor can the Russians send in enough technicians to dominate modernization. At a pinch, the Russians can send technicians to Korea and Mongolia, but the indications are that they usually serve for rather short terms, because the pressure is so great to get them back to

Russia to work on jobs where they are badly needed.

In this respect America competes at an advantage with Russia. America alone has plenty of technicians to export. They swarm in Iran, Afghanistan, and the Arab countries. One of the most effective services of the State Department is the "men wanted" bureau through which it finds and hires technical men of all kinds to go out and work for the governments of undeveloped countries. These men are good political agents. They convince many people in the countries in which they work that if only their own governments were more like that of America, there would be nothing that such wonder-working men could not accomplish. A recent survey showed that, except for countries like Northern Korea and Mongolia, whose governments are closely associated with that of Russia, the Russians had placed only two men of this kind in Asia — in a hospital in the Near East.

Limitations of this kind on the power of Russia are important. Too many Americans appear to believe as devoutly as the Russians, but more blindly, in the inevitability of the march of Communism in Asia. A mysterious potency is ascribed to "ideas" exported from Russia and to "Russian-trained" political organizers. The truth is that there is no shortage of bright ideas in Asia. Indonesia, Malaya, Burma, Indo-China, and China itself show that Russian-trained organizers are not needed either to start revolution or to keep it going; and that where they do appear they are no guarantee of success.

Indonesia is an example. In spite of Dutch propaganda, Communist influence in Indonesia was rather negligible, until the return from Russia of Muso in 1948. Muso was not a Communist because he was Russian-trained. He became a Communist, and got Russian training, because as a nationalist he fled from Indonesia about twenty years ago with a Dutch price on his head. In 1948 he returned to Indonesia, fortified by about twenty years of Russian training, but weakened by more than twenty years of lack of contact with his own people, and lack of knowledge of the channels in which Indonesian nationalism is now running. He started an insurrection within the Indonesian Republic, in an attempt to take over control from the more moderate nationalists. The result was to increase disunity. The Republic put down the Communists, but was itself so weakened that it cracked when the Dutch, dishonestly accusing it of being dominated by Communists, attacked it with planes and mechanized forces. Indonesian resistance to the Dutch will now turn to guerrilla warfare. Communists will probably win control of the leadership — not Russian-trained Communists, but militant nationalists who begin to call themselves Communists because the hard-faced Dutch in charge of military operations have convinced them that men who are going to be shot down as if they were Communists might as well organize themselves as Communists.

Whether China will bring out the strength or the weakness of the Russian position in Asia is a question that will be considered in Chapter VIII. One aspect of the question, however, should be touched on here.

The strength of the Chinese Communists lies in the fact that they have been able to develop, out of their own resources and the forces at work in China, the largest-scale Communist revolution in history outside of Russia itself. They have done this with virtually no Russian military aid. (The Japanese arms they acquired in Manchuria were more than matched by the Japanese arms turned over to Chiang Kai-shek by America and by the Japanese themselves.)

More important is the fact that, as pointed out in Chapter III, they have had no aid from Russia representing the productive power of modern industry. Both the limitations of Russian power and the limitations of European and American power in Asia are framed on the end-paper map. The debatable lands that lie between the Soviet land frontier and the ring of beachheads held by Europe and America are going to have their own political future. The trend of that future is going to be decided only in part by Russian, European, and American power. In part it is going to be decided by a balance between the repellent and attractive characteristics of Russian policy and the repellent and attractive characteristics of the policies of America and the European countries backed by America. The negative factor of repulsion will be as important as the positive factor of attraction.

The analysis of the politics of repulsion is much neglected by statesmen who do not seem to realize that it is a commodity in which they deal from day to day. It may be that more peoples have advanced backward into the future than have marched boldly forward;

backward, because their faces were turned toward
something which they resisted, and from which they
were defending themselves. There was certainly something of this phenomenon in the American Revolution. There was a great deal of it in the Russian Revolution, when many patriotic Russians, turning their
faces to the alien intervention on their soil, from which
they tried to defend themselves, found themselves
backed into Bolshevism. The same phenomenon has
been important in the recent history of Asia, and
most important of all in the history of the civil war
in China. The mixture of harsh oppression, incompetence, and scandalous corruption in the Kuomintang, rather than the wiles of Russian Communists or
the eloquence of Chinese Communists, has been the
chief recruiting agent of the Communist cause in
China.

In the long run, it is likely that America and Russia,
in the shares that they take in determining the future
of politics in Asia, will not succeed or fail so much by
the brilliant improvisations they make in seizing opportunities as by the mistakes they may make, or the
insensitivity they may show, in the routine conduct of
policy.

In the range of political ideas, there is very little
that the Russians can pretend to reveal to the peoples
of Asia that they do not know already. Even in the
range of political methods and practice many of the
peoples of Asia, such as the Chinese, the peoples of
Viet Nam, and the peoples of Indonesia, are probably learning faster than the Russians could teach

them. In military action the biggest single battle in
Asia, that of China, has already been won by the
Chinese Communists with little or no aid from Russia.
In the big battles that are being fought in colonial
Southeast Asia, it is practically impossible for Russia
to give military aid. In the fighting that may break
out in the Near East it will be difficult for Russia to
give aid on a large scale at any great distance from
her own frontiers without the danger of bringing on
a world war.

What is going to count, and heavily, is the ability to
give economic aid. Economically, the Soviet Union
is heavy and slow. Its economic strength is not of a
kind that is easily exported across its own frontiers.
In this field, America holds the initiative. America's
economic strength is of a kind that makes it possible
to send economic aid to great distances and in the
concentrated form which quickly creates new productive power in the countries aided. By giving economic
aid to some countries and withholding it from others,
America can bring to bear a kind of influence that is
scarcely, as yet, within the reach of Russia.

America and the European countries backed by
America hold a ring of bases and footholds around
Asia. If, using those positions of advantage, American
economic power and the threat of American military
power are used in an attempt to break or bend the
will of the peoples of Asia, most of those peoples will
be able to hold their ground geographically, but politically they will retreat into alliance with Russia.
Even with the great preponderance of strength that

we have at present, and with the frequent temptation to penalize economically countries which do not yield to us politically, we cannot afford to gamble with time. Before long, Russia's power of political attraction may revive and exercise a greater pull, especially on Asia, than it did in the 1930's.

For the time being Russia's range of economic action is geographically limited, and the amount of economic effort that Russia can make, even within that limited range, is not great. By 1952 there may be a great shift. We have been warned that by that year, which will mark the completion of the Marshall Plan program, Europe will still be below par economically and not able to stand firmly on its own feet. A lot will depend on whether Asia then is still holding out against the return of Western imperialism; and the probabilities are that colonial Asia cannot be reconquered, and China cannot be coerced. By 1952, on the other hand, the war wounds of Russia will be entirely healed. We must count on a rapid increase in Soviet economic strength from then on. If Russia should be able to put a considerably increased economic effort into Asia, the balance of the world is going to swing heavily in Russia's favor.

CHAPTER VI

JAPAN IS NOBODY'S ALLY

AMERICAN policy in Japan is based on the assumption that as Japan goes, so Asia can be made to go. The first link in the chain of assumption is that Japan can be made the workshop of Asia and a bulwark against Russia. This assumption is based on the marvelous theory that Japan, as an instrument of American policy, combines all the virtues of Britain, Germany, and the Kingdom of Nepal. Like Britain, it is to be used as a stationary aircraft carrier. Like Germany, it is superior in industrial development to all the countries near it, and therefore like Germany it is to be made the center from which the industrial development of the mainland near it is co-ordinated, controlled, and oriented against Russia. Like the Kingdom of Nepal, which is independent of India and furnishes fierce mercenary Gurkha warriors to both India and Britain, the "naturally disciplined" people of Japan, who are "traditionally anti-Russian," are expected, as time goes on, to furnish tough colonial legions of a new kind which, having no politics of their own, will be solidly loyal to the America which supports their homeland "workshop."

The first link in this chain of assumptions is the entirely fanciful theory that Japan can be made not only into a workshop, but a workshop that controls Asia. The second is the equally fanciful theory that Japan can be made into a politically reliable bulwark against Russia. The third is the most fanciful theory of all: that there is only one Japan, a solid, internally indivisible unit, like one Republican, or one trained seal.

This whole chain of assumptions and cluster of fantasies is an illusion. The illusion was born out of the stunned docility with which the Japanese accepted surrender. After the fanatic, bitter-end ferocity with which the Japanese had fought throughout the South Pacific and at Tarawa and on Okinawa, it was thought that this unbelievably sudden and complete meekness could only be explained by the "inherent sense of discipline" of the Japanese when the Emperor ordered them to surrender. The growth of the illusion was fostered by the precise, clockwork efficiency with which General MacArthur took over. He did, probably, the best job of its kind that has ever been done. The illusion grew to full stature during the first period of General MacArthur's administration, which ran from the surrender in August 1945 until the 80th Congress was elected in the United States in 1946.

In this period an American New Deal was carried out in Japan. With the touch of fatherly mysticism that he combines with his old-line Republicanism, General MacArthur salted New Dealers all through SCAP, his headquarters organization as Supreme Commander for the Allied Powers. It is true that there were never many at the very top; but there were a great many in the middle ranks, which in any bureaucracy are all-important. They were especially influential in the drafting of policy, with the result that even in this period policies were usually more progressive and New Dealish in the form in which they were announced than in the form in which they were carried out.

Some of the New Dealers were civilian officers who had been commissioned during the war. Some came straight from Washington after the surrender, when SCAP in Tokyo, desperately short of experienced bureaucrats, was squalling for help just at the time that President Truman, in his first pathetic attempt to appease the Republicans in the name of "unity," was junking New Dealers as fast as they could be nudged out of the way by the cold-shoulder treatment. The irony of this migration from Washington to Tokyo recalled the good old days when America shipped so much scrap iron to Japan that there was a shortage of scrap in America itself.

Portentous changes began when the 80th Congress was elected in America. As its first war whoops were borne on the air waves to Tokyo, its tribal kinsmen on General MacArthur's staff began to gather in powwows of their own. The scalps of the pale-faced New Dealers began to come loose. There was a purge. The cleverest — and crookedest — of the old-line Japanese politicians caught on. Recovering their poise and agility, they made new bids. Get Japan off the neck of the American taxpayer? Nothing easier, they said with perfectly straight faces. If only the American taxpayer would stick his neck a long, long way out, they would get off it. They would make Japan an ally, a workshop, a bulwark.

Many of the facts of these changes, and most of their significance, were obscured from American public opinion. General MacArthur's hat was big enough to hide Japan under it. The publicity arrangements were such that Japan could talk only through General MacArthur's hat. General MacArthur is a first-class administrator. His machine of administration functioned efficiently. It was particularly efficient in all matters in which the old-line Japanese politicians working with it wanted to help it to be efficient.

General MacArthur and SCAP have found it easy to win a cordial response from the American press and public opinion because a number of the very important aspects of efficiency are favored by the fact that America is virtually in sole occupation of Japan. Only token numbers of British Empire troops share the military occupation. Exactly the right screen of internationalism is provided by an Inter-Allied Advisory Council in Tokyo and a Far Eastern Commission of eleven nations in Washington to draft policy directives. General MacArthur's real powers are doubly safeguarded by the American tradition that a commander in the field has the widest latitude in interpreting the directives under which he works, and by a Washington ruling that in the event of differences of opinion "the policies of the United States will govern." [1]

The combined structure of policy and administration is able to keep the Russians on the side lines. Having no power of veto, and no share in the military occupation of Japan, as they have in Germany, they can be regularly outvoted at the policy level and, after being outvoted, have no power to obstruct at the administrative level. They can only stand on the side lines and protest. In the short run, this has been a great advantage to American policy. It has contributed immeasurably to the working efficiency of the American occupation, and in the psychological aspects of the cold war it has made it possible to present the Russians as would-be troublemakers, fortunately held in restraint by the wise hand of General MacArthur.

In the long run, these temporary advantages may prove to have been illusory. In the long run, it will prove impossible to determine the future of Japan apart from the future of Asia as a whole. The future of Asia as a whole is not likely to be determined either by the positive power of majority votes or by the negative veto power of any one great nation. It is much more likely to be determined by a complicated series of concessions and compromises, leading at last to workable agreement. Between now and the long-term settlement, which is not likely to be reached for

---

[1] "U. S. Initial Post-Surrender Policy for Japan," jointly prepared by the Department of State, War Department, and Navy Department and sent to General MacArthur August 29, 1945; approved by President Truman September 6, 1945.

some years, the present American policy in Japan is likely to turn very, very sour. If that should happen, it would be a great embarrassment to have the Russians able to say "We told you so," while America is unable to retort, "You were in it too."

In the development of the whole situation, and in the widening gap between the realities of Japan and the illusory picture of Japan that has been built up in America, General MacArthur's personal public-relations setup has been of incalculable importance. No American general has ever had public-relations henchmen who were so fast on their feet or so slow in the head. Their creed is that General MacArthur should be represented not only as a source of great wisdom, which he is, but as the only source of unerring wisdom, which he is not. It is a tragedy that this should be so, because when the mirage breaks down General MacArthur's high and deserved place in history is likely to be damaged. He is a general of genius, an extremely capable administrator, a great statesman, and potentially a very great statesman. His one weakness, which has prevented him from realizing his full potential as a statesman, is his inability to keep sycophants out of his entourage.

The truth is that the present "realistic" policy in Japan is going to fail, because it is not in fact realistic but pseudo-realistic. The truth is that there have in recent history been several Japans. There is the Japan that we defeated. There is the interim Japan of the New Deal period between V–J Day in August 1945 and the election of the 80th Congress in the fall of

1946. There is the Japan that American policy has aimed at creating through 1947 and 1948 and still hopes to create. And, finally, there is the real Japan of today. This real Japan is unstable in its internal composition. It is likely to blow up in our faces. If it does, the explosion will in some ways be like an atomic bomb, with poisonous radioactive effects on our interests and policies in Asia, and in some ways like a humiliating stink bomb, damaging the reputations of General MacArthur and of policy makers in Washington.

The Japan that we defeated has always been presented to the American public as a Japan stunned by the atomic bombs dropped on Hiroshima and Nagasaki, but still disciplined in its reflexes and responsive to the Emperor's command to surrender, which saved untold American casualties. The realities are somewhat different. Japan could have been defeated, and was ready to surrender, without the atomic bomb. The rulers of Japan were looking for a way to surrender the nation while saving themselves. If the atomic bombs had not been dropped, another excuse would have been found. It is widely believed, not only in Russia but in Europe — see Professor Blackett's uncomfortable book on the whole atomic problem [2] — that the atomic bombs were not in fact dropped because there was no other way of clinching the surrender of Japan, but as a warning to Russia that we had become able to defeat Japan without Russia's

[2] P. M. S. Blackett, *Fear, War, and the Bomb*, New York, 1949.

intervention in Manchuria, which we had previously
been so overeager to secure; and that, having this
weapon at last in our hands, we were henceforth on
totally different terms not only with Japan, but with
Russia itself.

There is in fact no justification whatever for believing that there was any "Russian angle" to the
dropping of atomic bombs on Japan. There is every
reason for believing that President Truman, who made
the final decision and took on himself the sole responsibility for it, was guided only by the feeling
that it was his duty to bring the war to an end as
quickly as possible, with the loss of as few American
lives as possible. But from the moment that the first
of the bombs was dropped, the number of Russians
who might be atomically destroyed became politically
more important than the number of Japanese who had
been disintegrated.

Immediately after the dropping of the bombs it was
officially announced that the atomic weapon represented a totally new military potential. "Atomic thinking" at once began to dominate Washington. It would
be absurd to suppose that it took any longer for the
rulers of Japan to figure out that if the bombing of
Hiroshima and Nagasaki could be used to stop the war
before the Russians got any nearer, the existence of the
atom bomb in America's hands might later be converted into a shield over Japan to keep the Russians
out permanently. The rulers of Japan were maneuvering to find a way of surrendering that would leave
them with some of their old power within the country.

Their only hope was conflict of policy among the victors, and especially between America and Russia. By using the bombs as a reason for surrendering promptly, they could end the war with the power position and the advantage of prestige all over the Far East heavily in America's favor. If they hesitated, the surge of the Russian advance through Manchuria would within a week or two immeasurably improve the Soviet position. They did not hesitate.

The Japan that was ready for surrender, with or without the atom bomb, was being held together in those last days by fear, not by loyalty to the Emperor. The avalanche of disaster had already been great enough to sweep away awe for the godlike being in whose name and for whose glory the Japanese had been hurled into war, and to replace it with hatred. The priority of fear was the only thing that gave people no time to stop, scratch their heads, and say, with the wonderment of recognition: "The Emperor is a louse!" It can be said with certainty that the prestige of the Emperor had in fact become so hollow that only a thin outer veneer remained uncracked. Immediately after the surrender it threatened to crack. Scurrilous jokes about him began to circulate openly; there was disaffection even within the Imperial Guard, and if there had been any signs of American indifference there would have been public demonstrations against him. What saved the Emperor was General MacArthur's skill in treating him with just the right amount of dignity over and above what was required by correct protocol, and the clear American intention that he should be retained as the symbolic head of state.

The fear that held priority in Japan in the last weeks before surrender was the fear that the Americans would land like ravening savages, slaughtering men, women, and children. This fear made it seem better to die like brave Japanese, facing the beaches, than to submit and be slaughtered. It was not the authority of the Emperor, ordering surrender, that quelled this fear, but the instinctive knowledge of a people who had never in all their history had an order from an Emperor that was not for the good of the Emperor. If the Emperor ordered surrender, he must have fixed things up.

Once MacArthur had shown after the landing that his troops were under better discipline than the Japanese had ever known among their own troops, there was a shaky period in which the revulsion of feeling made admiration for the Americans paramount over respect for the Emperor or any of the other old symbols of authority. With an admirable feel for the right combination of firmness and condescension toward a people who had always been used to authority and who were emotionally shattered by defeat, General MacArthur steadied this feeling and guided it into the channels of his New Deal period.

In this period the representatives of the old authority were given the fright of their lives, but gradually allowed to understand that the Americans would not let the wrath of the people work up to a full head of steam. The people were given to understand that the Americans would grant them a lot more democracy than they had ever had before, but that they had better not try to win any democracy for themselves above and beyond what was prescribed in the SCAP directives. Political jails were opened. Even Communists were let out. Labor unions were allowed to assert themselves once more. There was liberty of the press, radio, the theater, public speech, and assembly to a degree altogether surprising under a military occupation of a defeated country.

Eager New Deal beavers slapped together a new constitution which was to be the ark of the new covenant of democracy. General MacArthur took great personal interest in it. Several passages of rich, beautiful prose, including a total renunciation of war and of the right to maintain armed forces, standing out like the phrases in capital letters in a Hearst editorial, were universally ascribed to the General himself. It was — of course — officially a Japanese constitution, promulgated not by SCAP but by the Japanese authorities. Japanese delicately intimated that they knew what the score was by circulating the story, after the Japanese text had been published, "What do you think of the new constitution?" "I don't know; I can't read English." And indeed, there were many passages extremely difficult to translate into intelligible Japanese.

In spite of its inevitable touches of irony and bathos, this was a good period. Real democracy cannot be given. It must be earned, and won against opposition. Above all, it is impossible to "give" democracy under an alien military occupation. What General MacArthur really gave to the Japanese people — and it was

the best and wisest thing in his power to give them —
was a schooling in the practices of democracy. They
were allowed to act as if they had won and created
some of the basic rights and duties of democracy.
They were put through their paces. The difference
between all this and real democracy is like the difference between taking the subway to a riding school
in Manhattan and being turned loose with a horse in
Montana and told to find your own way to Arizona;
but the practice was invaluable for a people who will
one day sign a peace treaty and see the occupation
end, and will then have to find their way from their
own Montana to their own Arizona.

Then came the period in which policies in Tokyo
echoed first the approach and then the arrival of the
80th Congress. The equivalent of the end of price
controls in America was permission for American
businessmen to take advantage of the American government's practical monopoly of control over Japan
to resume private enterprise. The costs of occupation
were paid by the taxpayer (though nominally charged
to the Japanese government, to be paid in some un-
known future). Any profits that could be made by
private enterprise stayed private. In order that the
government, in the public interest, should determine
the proper scope of business interest, influential businessmen were assigned to one official mission after another and sent out to Japan.

The equivalent of the Taft-Hartley Act was a
tightened control of labor unions. Strikes which the
unions were likely to lose were of course permitted.

Important strikes which the unions might have won were called off by administrative order. The program for breaking up the Zaibatsu, the great combined vertical and horizontal trusts, was put in the icebox. There was even an equivalent of the Un-American Activities Committee. The Counter-Intelligence service combed out surviving New Dealers and bounced them back to America.

In this period it became evident that the society of Japan is still, like the society of Germany, a sick society. Imperialism, like fascism, is a disease that bites deep. Those who wish to cure it simply by drafting well-worded constitutions and circulating some improving literature should face the facts. The grip that imperialism or fascism gets on a people depends on whether they get anything out of it. For decades, long before Pearl Harbor, a lot of Japanese got a lot out of imperialism. Formosa, Korea, and later Manchuria provided not only big profits for big shots, but jobs and the interest of travel and the feeling of belonging to a superior people for hundreds of thousands of Japanese who otherwise would never have had anything but the humblest employment. Engineers, technicians, newspaper correspondents, and traveling salesmen benefited as well as army officers. The feeling grew that the Japanese were entitled to be better off than their neighbors, and to have their neighbors pay for it.

In their post-surrender New Deal period the Japanese took their new democracy seriously, because that was the period in which it seemed most certain that they were going to have to work their own passage into the future. They could not do so unless they abandoned the feelings of superiority and privilege. In the 80th Congress period the old disease came back on them because the American emphasis on the American interest in making Japan the workshop of Asia and a bulwark against Russia seemed to assure them once more of a higher position in life than the one they actually earned: the Americans would support them in the style of life to which they had become accustomed while lording it over the Formosans, the Koreans, and the Chinese.

It is with this feeling well revived and going strong that the 80th Congress period of American policy in Japan has merged into the present period. Our policy now aims at creating a Japan which is to be the counterpart in Asia of the kind of Germany we are trying to create in Europe. It is to be less and less a conquered enemy, a ward, or even an instrument of policy, and to become more and more an overt ally. As the workshop of Asia, it is to be closely integrated with America, so that American economic policy will flow unobstructed through Japan into the rest of Asia. As an ally, it is to be not only an ally against Russia, but an ally taking precedence over China, our own former ally and Japan's former enemy, in which we are now so sadly disappointed — just as we put great faith in the anti-Russianness of Germany, and are suspicious of France, where Communism is too strong for our liking and where the workers, not being as dependent on us for their food as are the German workers, are less docile.

We have traveled along a double line in reaching the present stage of American policy. The mutations of policy inside Japan have just been described. In addition, there is an aspect of American policy that envelops Japan from the outside and links it with American policy toward Russia and on the mainland of Asia. This external policy has also had its changes.

Under the concept of policy that prevailed at the war's end, Japan was regarded as a dangerous enemy which had been defeated with great difficulty. It was realized that even in defeat Japan remained industrially the most powerful nation in Asia. In spite of war damage, Japan's engineers could rebuild Japanese industry faster than other nations in Asia, short of engineers and managerial personnel, could build new industries and get them going. Japan's knowledge of foreign trade, banking, shipping, and insurance was also a reservoir of power to be reckoned with. It was then still the prevailing opinion that Russia would be economically prostrate for the first few years after the war, would need American aid to ease the terrible strain, and consequently would on the whole be manageable in the United Nations. It seemed wise, therefore, to insure against a too rapid revival of Japanese power.

It was thought that the policy that suited the situation would be to keep Japan's postwar recovery under strict control but to do so as part of a broader policy of hastening the economic development and recovery of the rest of Asia. The Zaibatsu should be broken up. Japan should not be allowed a head start in the postwar market. Highly specialized war industries should be taken out of Japan altogether, or destroyed. Industry surplus to a reasonable maintenance standard of living should be taken out and allocated to Japan's neighbors. Japan's huge surplus of machine tools, which are one of the key factors in all modern industry and which in small units can also be made serviceable in starting up new industries in undeveloped countries, should also be distributed to other countries in Asia.

This view may be summed up by saying that since the American occupation could not be made indefinite, and since it would be difficult to keep effective control over Japan from a distance, the rational safeguard would be to make Japan's neighbors in Asia strong enough to stand as sentinels. Against strong enough neighbors, Japan could not resume aggression. This view was later modified less by the strength and toughness of Russia — though Russia made the best talking point — than by the increasing evidence that the governments which America supported for political reasons in China, the Philippines, and later in South Korea, were hopelessly incompetent when it came to quick or efficient economic reconstruction. In addition colonial Asia was already in turmoil and India was doggedly negotiating and maneuvering its way toward dominion status and partition between the Union of India and Pakistan.

The early view faded out rapidly. It was replaced by the view that the next menace to Asia as a whole would not be a revived Japan after all, but a Russia which had somehow not been bled white by the German war. This fear was quickly reinforced by the fear of revolutions all over Asia which might turn in sympathy toward Russia.

The new problem of Russia, or the problem of Russia in its new form, could have been dealt with in two ways.

Every single government in Asia to which we were politically friendly (with the partial exception of the first postwar government of Siam) was a bad government. The colonial governments were passionately hated by the peoples over whom they were trying to reassert their authority, and it was doubtful whether they could impose their authority by force, even with considerable aid. The governments of China, the Philippines, and later South Korea, were controlled by men who had a lust for power and a greed for money but no intention to satisfy the demands of their peoples for less dictatorship and more representative government.

Even Chiang Kai-shek, a genuine war hero whose country had resisted Japan longer than any other, was surrounded by a Byzantine palace guard of knaves and fools and was disregarding the reforms recommended by Americans and Chinese as his best weapons of political warfare. If the demands of other Chinese for more democracy and representative government were an aid and comfort to the Communists, then they must be crushed too. The people must be obedient to the government. When they had been reduced to docile obedience the government might, if it saw fit, gradually grant rights which would perhaps, in the distant future, enable the people to place their own representatives in the government.

The first alternative, in an over-all policy toward Asia, would have been to allow the fall of any government which met with so much internal resistance that, without American support, it was bound either to fall or to make big compromises. The process of fall could have been eased, compromise encouraged, and chaotic collapse prevented, if American mediation of a Marshall mission kind had been offered in other countries than China. One reason why the Marshall mission failed in China in 1945–1946, after coming so near to success, was the fact that it was the only mission of its kind. All Chinese felt instinctively, in spite of the integrity of General Marshall himself, that the mission was an emergency attempt to patch things up temporarily and did not represent a general and sustained American policy.

If there had been such a general American policy, newly emerging governments, parties, and movements claiming the right of representation could have been met with an American cordiality adapted, in each case, to the strength of the trend toward representative government, constructive and progressive economic policies, degree of popular support, and any other signs indicating the filling of the political vacuum solidly enough to discourage the penetration of Communism. Within such a general policy, the early New Deal trend in Japan could have been continued, on the safe assumption that the reform movement in Japan would be welcomed by reform movements all over

Asia, and that a general trend of this kind would serve both to check Communism and to prevent the recovery of aggressive militarism in Japan.

This alternative was not followed. The alternative that was followed was determined by the fact that too many stomachs in Washington had pits in them, and too many of these pits were hollow with the queasy feeling that any rapid and general change in Asia must somehow be more to the interest of Communism and Russia than to the interest of America. To make themselves feel more solid, the queasy stomachs wanted first of all to steady the whirling world. They did not demand authoritarian governments, but they wanted strong governments so much that they were prepared to find excuses for authoritarian governments. First of all they urged, as a practical issue, that governments must be helped to "restore order." After that it would be time enough to allow the question of the control of peoples over governments to come up — as a debating issue. If strong governments were strong enough internally to assert control over their peoples, but weak enough externally to be forced to look to America for support and therefore for guidance, that surely was of no detriment to the American interest.

It was easy for this drift to merge with the growing conviction that it was necessary to set up a "containment" of Russia, in order to have a whip hand in coming to a general agreement with Russia, and easy for both tendencies to merge into the concept of using Japan, firmly under American control, as both a workshop for Asia and a bulwark against Russia. As drift merged with drift to become a set course of policy, two characteristics of politics in Asia were edged into the dim background of thought and there forgotten.

The first of these characteristics is that any government in Asia that is more dependent on American support than on the support of its own people is certain to convince the people that the American determination to contain Russia is victimizing them in a way that will make them suffer, whether America succeeds or not. They become convinced that they are being made satellites, not allies, and that their government, instead of representing them, has become a stooge and a puppet. They are then prepared to believe that American policy is in fact a new imperialism, politically determined to stop the growth of representative government and economically determined to create new colonies in Asia to be exploited by American big business.

The second important characteristic of politics in Asia was pointed out in Chapter II. No necessity ties Japan down to be America's permanent ally in Asia. A Japan made strong enough by American subsidy to hold an economic ascendancy over the rest of Asia, and strong enough to be an American ally against Russia if it wants to be, is automatically a Japan strong enough to double-cross America and make its own deals both with Russia and with the rest of Asia. It is true that Japan must be included in the eventual balance to be struck between the American interest in Asia and the Russian interest. But it is equally true that America cannot force the striking of that balance by trying to make Japan or any other single country in Asia the primary instrument of American policy. The general stabilization that will eventually emerge between America and Russia will in large part be brought about by the realization that Asia cannot be brought fully under the control of either of them. It is unwise to overlook the historical part played by Japan in transforming an Asia under control into an Asia out of control. There are Japanese who realize that Japan will only be able to become free by taking its place — not a dominant place — in an Asia out of the control of either of the two superpowers.

It is in this light that we must study the real Japan that underlies all the other partly historical, partly transitory, and partly illusory Japans. This real Japan is undergoing internal changes. More than one outcome is possible. Our policy problem therefore ranges beyond "what to do with Japan." We must also think of the effects *in* Japan of our policy *about* Japan.

Unlike Germany, Japan has no Ruhr. In attempting to make Japan the workshop of Asia and a bulwark against Russia, there are certain advantages that we can exploit; but there are also serious deficiencies to be overcome. The balance sheet is not in our favor.

What Japan does not have is coking coal, iron, oil, bauxite for making aluminum, or the capacity to produce on a large scale some of the important agricultural raw materials for industry, such as cotton. Japan does not have enough salt to sustain its chemical industry or enough wood of the right kind to sustain its rayon industry; and both of these were formerly important earners of foreign exchange. In addition, of course, Japan has about a 20 per cent deficiency in food production; and this problem is aggravated by lack of fertilizers, which have to be imported.

What Japan does have is hydroelectric energy, one of the big requirements of both heavy and light industry; coal other than coking coal, though not enough of it, and silk. Japan's most important resources, however, are human: the most advanced and diversified technical and managerial know-how in Asia, and the largest pool of skilled industrial labor.

With these resources and in spite of these deficiencies Japan in fact was for a while the workshop of Asia. The use of military power was what bridged the deficiencies. By imperial control of Korea and Formosa, later of Manchuria, and for a while of much of China and all Indo-China, Siam, Malaya, Burma, and Netherlands India, Japan was able to plan the extraction of raw materials and to regulate processing and distribution. The form of control made it possible not only to obtain raw materials, but to dictate exchange values. Raw materials were extracted at colonial or coolie wage rates. When processed, one portion was set aside to maintain the military machine that kept the whole business going. Another was allocated to consumer goods for the countries that produced the raw materials. A third, before Pearl Harbor, went into world trade and earned dollars and pounds sterling.

The United States cannot put Japan back in business as this kind of workshop. America made enormous sacrifices to break Japan's imperial grip on Asia and

the Pacific. Even war scares about Russia are not
enough to make American public opinion reverse itself and demand an American reconquest, on Japan's
behalf, of Japan's old fields of aggression in Asia. War
scares about Russia inevitably stress the strategic
importance of Western Europe. It would be strategic
as well as political folly to send either American troops
or American-led Japanese troops against nationalist
resistance in Asia while Russian strength remains in
Russia, undispersed and uncommitted.

A program for making Japan once more a workshop
must depend either on American subsidies or on direct
agreements between Japan and parts of Asia which
America cannot control. Direct American grants to
Japan jumped from $96,000,000 in the fiscal year end-
ing June 30, 1946, to $292,000,000 in 1947 and $423,-
000,000 in 1948. In addition, loans and credits totaled
$116,000,000 in 1947 and $61,000,000 in the fiscal year
ending in 1948.[3] Adding the costs of actual military
occupation — which nominally are chargeable to the
Japanese government at some time in the future when
Japan becomes solvent — it is a reasonable estimate that
the total American expenditure on Japan, including
military costs, approaches a billion a year.[4] Japan now

[3] Bureau of Foreign and Domestic Commerce of the
U. S. Department of Commerce, *Survey of Current Business*,
November 1948.

[4] The attitude of General MacArthur's headquarters
toward the taxpayer's interest in military costs is revealed by
the report that Major-General H. J. Casey, army engineering
officer, when asked by the correspondent of a Chicago newspaper for some information about construction and occu-

gets its major imports of food and raw cotton from the United States, on a government basis. In 1947, 53 per cent of the value of Japan's imports was in grain and starch; 13 per cent in raw cotton; and 12 per cent in fertilizers. By 1948, Japan attained a favorable ratio of eight to one in its exports to the Orient as compared with imports from other countries, but was able to export to the United States only one twenty-fifth of the value of its imports from the United States.[5] These ratios indicate an increasing indebtedness to the United States, with no increase in the ability to pay off the debt, since the "soft currency" income from Japanese sales to Asia is not wanted by the United States.

Sums of money can always be juggled. The cost of food and cotton sent to Japan can, if it seems advisable in the interest of high policy, be charged to the cost of

pation costs in Japan, allegedly replied that the people of Chicago would not be interested in such details. — *San Francisco Chronicle*, June 25, 1948.

The difficulty of getting precise statements on occupation costs is not limited to the unwillingness of military spokesmen to give out information. The United States Budget is a document weighing nearly seven pounds. Details of expenditures are scattered through it in such a way that large-scale research is required to bring together the figures which belong under any such general heading as "cost of the occupation of Japan." It is a curious comment on the relationship between the taxes paid by the citizen and the information available to the citizen that a breakdown of the budget is in fact prepared, giving global totals of expenditure under inclusive headings; but it is circulated only to the President and a very few high officials.

[5] John E. Fields, "Far Eastern Trade — 1948," *Far Eastern Survey*, New York, September 22, 1948.

supporting U. S. farm prices instead of being charged to Japan. But in the end there are certain values that cannot be juggled, and that confront us with a dilemma. The rock-bottom value of American agricultural exports is based on American wages, the price received by the American farmer, and the margins of profit added as the goods pass from hand to hand — all in American dollars. Cutting these values would be cutting the American standard of living. But Japan used to obtain food and a great part of its cotton from Asia, in soft currencies, at prices geared to the lowest standards of living in the world.

Who is to pay the difference? Is Japan to be charged what its food and raw material imports actually cost in dollars, or only what they would have cost if purchased in Asia, with the difference being charged off to the American taxpayer? Sooner or later, if the first alternative is followed, the Japanese are going to squawk that they are being made bondslaves to the American standard of living. If the second alternative is followed, American taxpayers will make a political issue of the fact that we are supporting Japan indefinitely on a dole that increases from year to year.

The outcome of the Chinese civil war may make us face this dilemma soon. Until recently, Chiang Kai-shek held the railway hub of Mukden in Manchuria, while the Chinese Communists besieged it. With the railway cut, export traffic could not move to the great seaport of Dairen, where the Russians sat tight. The issue of whether Dairen should or should not be open to international trade, as stipulated by treaty, could not be raised in practical form. Now it can be raised. The Chinese Communists have stabilized their control both in Manchuria and in adjoining North China. Most of the rail net has been restored.

China will soon be in a position to make economic offers to Japan. The northeastern provinces (Manchuria), formerly so closely integrated with Japan, have a surplus of food to offer. Most of this surplus never was marketed in China; the established channels of trade do not run in that direction. There will be an over-all food deficiency in China until the 1949 harvests, because of the civil war; but after that, offering food to Japan would not cause hardships in China and make the new government unpopular, because wherever the Communists have taken over they have increased food production, controlled distribution, and stabilized prices, successfully breaking the old cycle of recurring shortages and famines. This food could be offered to Japan at prices much lower than food from America. Soybeans, of which there are big accumulated stocks, are useful for many industrial purposes, as well as for food. The cake that is left after pressing out the bean oil is of high value both as cattle feed and as fertilizer, of which Japan is desperately short.

More important still, the northern and northeastern provinces of China are traditionally Japan's greatest sources of iron and coking coal, and of salt for the chemical industry. Japan formerly used China's iron ore and coking coal to make first pig iron and then steel. An important variation on this pattern is now possible. China could offer pig iron and later, as the

Chinese iron and steel industries develop, semi-processed and processed iron and steel in various forms. In this way Japan could retain a useful and profitable steel and machine-building industry, which step by step could contribute to the industrialization of the rest of Asia. A high level of employment could be sustained, and a full scope of usefulness for Japan's managers and technicians. Yet Asia and the world would be secured against a revival of Japanese militarism and aggression because Japan would no longer control the sources of supply. By withholding raw ore and supplying Japan only with pig iron and other semi-processed materials, China would have absolute power to cut off the revival of Japanese war industry.

Moves and offers of this kind are now practical politics. Their political importance is sharpened by the fact that Japan, while under American control, is not a free agent. China can make offers which flatter the Japanese with the prospect of honorable economic interdependence, on terms of costs and prices that suit both countries. These offers can be worded in such a way that if Japan, under American control, is constrained to turn them down and to continue in a growing dependence on America and indebtedness to America, it will be very difficult for American policy to escape looking like a dog in the Japanese manger.

Such moves would affect the conditions under which both America and Russia maneuver for economic, political, and strategic advantage. They would also do more than that. They would promote new groupings in Japanese domestic politics. Both the labor union movement and the parties of the left would be able to press demands for friendly reintegration with Asia, based not simply on political sympathy but on arguments of solid economic advantage. The effort of the Japanese Communists to take over a large part of the membership of the Social Democrats would be strengthened. General MacArthur would find military occupation and administrative control less and less adequate for chastening the labor unions, manipulating political parties, and jockeying the Communists and the rest of the radical left out of position. America would slip from ascendancy over the whole of Japan to the awkward position of partisan support of the right in a divided Japan.

Rightist interests in Japan are already aware of these possibilities, and are preparing their countermoves. At the end of 1948 Tateko Horiuchi returned to Japan. During the war, he had held a high position in Occupied China. At the end of the war, like many other top civilian and military Japanese, he was taken over by the government of Chiang Kai-shek, and served as an advisor to T. V. Soong in South China and the ancestral Soong island of Hainan, which since the war, with American aid, has been an important supplier of iron ore to Japan. (Since the function of such Japanese had been to make themselves the masters of the Chinese people, the use of them by the Kuomintang after the war was one of the things that infuriated public opinion and undermined support for Chiang Kai-shek, because of the implication that a government that would use such people must itself be more eager to take over control of the people than to represent the people.)

On his return to Japan Horiuchi trotted out a different kind of proposal for economic integration between Japan and China.[6] Japan, in his view, should favor an end to the civil war in China, through political compromise. The rehabilitation of Japan itself should then be geared to an economic program in South China and especially in Hainan Island, where "there is much room left for Japanese technicians to utilize their experiences in the development of the island." Instead of confining itself to the export of textiles and other consumer goods, Japan should take part in a program of industrialization, centered in South China, that would help China to become self-sufficient.

This proposal represents the conservative interest in Japan. Turning its back on Russia and on the traditional "doorstep" position of Japan in Manchuria and North China, it looks toward the southern coast of China and toward Southeast Asia, which lies beyond. Horiuchi's proposal reveals the subtlety and flexibility with which the old big business interests of Japan are working for a comeback.

Without giving any hint that they might, if it ever suits them, refuse to let Japan be used as America's vanguard against Russia, these interests will as time passes steadily build up the emphasis on America's obligation to protect them from Russia. By advocating a shift of Japan's interest from North China to South

[6] Radio Tokyo, in Japanese to Japan, December 29, 1948.

China they will put themselves in a position to co-operate with America — for a few years, at any rate — if America should experiment with a policy of support-ing a rump anti-Communist Chinese government on the islands of Formosa and Hainan, with a few foot-holds perhaps along the South China coast.

When Japan's conservatives look south they see be-yond South China. By the time the end of the war forced them out of colonial Southeast Asia they saw perfectly clearly what the next phase of colonial politics was going to be like and what opportunities it held for them. Japanese conservatives and leftists have one thing in common. They realize that as a de-feated and occupied nation, Japan has a long and rough road to travel to get back to independence and free-dom of action in international politics. As a country of this kind, situated in Asia, Japan is like the colonial countries which are struggling to get as much inde-pendence as they can from a Europe backed by America.

It is dangerous for America to overlook this fact. There is an important area of political maneuver in which Japanese conservatives and leftists and right-wing and left-wing colonial nationalists can all get to-gether. As maneuvering goes on, it will be perfectly possible for Japan to emerge, suddenly and without warning, and with the hearty participation of some of the most powerful Japanese conservatives, in a position more anti-American than anti-Russian. Once the occu-pation of Japan has ended it will be possible for Japan to make such a move at any moment when it appears that the combined strength of Japan and the colonial peoples has reached a point where they can form a solid front against an American-backed Europe. The move, when made, might either be permitted without interference from Russia and China, or actually be assisted by them.

America is pre-eminently the country that has a head-on power conflict with Russia. The other countries, even when they are supposedly on the American side, do not have exactly the same kind of conflict with Russia. They are caught in between. If they cannot get out of the way, they may suffer least by staying on the American side. If they can get out of the way, they may suffer less by getting out of the way. Because of the difference in the nature of the conflict, Americans are inclined to insist that the ideology of Russian politics is absolute, rigid, and driven on by a conviction of fate and predestination. People in Europe and Asia, even very conservative people, are much more inclined to accept the kind of relativity in Russian and Communist ideology that was illustrated in Chapter IV: the willingness to be satisfied with a "step forward" even when it is not a step forward all the way to the control of a state by a Communist party.

Many intermediate steps forward of this kind may be taken in Asia in the next ten, twenty, or even fifty years that will satisfy Russia if they merely mean a weakening of the European and American power structure, without putting control into Russia's own hands. Russia was quite satisfied when Kemal Ataturk carried Turkey a step forward in this direction in the

1920's, removing Turkey from the control of Britain without coming under the control of Russia.

An Asia out of control may settle into a new position in world politics during the next few decades by a series of landslips, each causing a series of alarming tremors, but no general earthquake. During one or another of these landslips Japan, after talking a wonderful anti-Russian line up to the very last moment, and after getting every possible kind of help out of America, may see an opening which makes it possible to slip out from under America's control without coming under Russia's control. And Russian policy, for decades to come, may be guided by the belief that if it is possible for any part of Asia to break away from European or American control, but not possible to bring it either under Russian control or into a federation dominated by Russia, then it is wisest to settle for an Asia out of control.

The mere possibility of such developments affects the American interest in Japan and American policy toward Japan as a part of Asia. The possibility that as Japan goes so Asia can be made to go is in fact a decreasing possibility. The increasing probability is that as Asia goes, so Japan will go — in its alignments with other countries and in the alignments and oppositions of its own political parties.

CHAPTER VII

WAR AND REVOLUTION
IN CHINA

IN ALL Asia, China is the country farthest beyond control by America, Russia, or Europe, and the least likely to be brought under control. This uncontrollability results from the way in which the Second World War was fought and from the course then followed by the civil war in China itself.

In 1937, when the struggle for survival against Japan began, China was controlled by the Kuomintang, a party which owed nothing to elections or to representative forms of government, and which itself appointed not only the national government but provincial governments and even the administrative officials of counties. In parts of the country where its power was unchallenged, the Kuomintang made such appointments without consulting anybody. In regions where its power was weaker, it accepted and confirmed appointments made by whoever was in power locally; but the local power was also of a self-appointed kind, under control by no process of elected representative government.

During the war this government, headed by Chiang

Kai-shek, was driven into the deep hinterland. The Japanese occupied nearly half of the country, including most of the highly productive and densely populated regions. In Free China Chiang Kai-shek hung on grimly in a purely defensive war described officially as "trading space for time." Within Free China, the Kuomintang tightened all controls, pushing its authority from the top right down into the villages. The alternative of stimulating patriotic enthusiasm by calling for popular elections and building a pyramid of representative government from the grass roots up to the apex occupied by Chiang Kai-shek himself was rejected. It was considered that the people were politically immature, and that representative government would only throw into confusion the discipline needed for carrying on the war.

This policy was guided by the forecast, which proved to be correct, that Japan was bound to come into conflict either with America and Britain or with Russia, that it would then be defeated, and that as a by-product of the victory over Japan of some other power or powers China would recover full control over its own territory. It was assumed that the recovered territories would be in disorder. To restore order as quickly as possible, it would be necessary to step in at once with disciplined men to be placed in all key posts. The Kuomintang accordingly busied itself throughout the war with intensive Party training. Personnel of all kinds — officers, bureaucrats, bankers, businessmen, professional men, landlords — were selected in rotation and put through intensive training schools. The course of training was heavily influenced by fascist theories, and by the methods of Hitler more than those of Mussolini. It included rigid drilling in the dogma of "One Country, One Party, One Leader," and in disciplined, automatic acceptance of orders coming down the "chain of command." Initiative at lower levels was treated as subversive.

In Occupied China, the Japanese retorted with a Machiavellian program of counterfeiting the Kuomintang itself. Respectable Chinese precedents for submission to authority were culled from the Confucian literature. These were blended with suitable excerpts from the literature of the Kuomintang. A government of collaborators was set up, controlled by Japanese "advisors" and "experts," but headed by the traitor Wang Ching-wei, who had once been one of the most popular and flamboyantly "nationalist" heroes of the Kuomintang. Titles and nominal functions in the puppet structure closely imitated those in the Kuomintang and heavily favored the more prosperous urban classes, the landlords, and the richer peasants. It is considered unpatriotic in China, quite naturally, to admit how effectively this Japanese program worked.

The Kuomintang appeal to disciplined patriotism and blind obedience was ineffective in undermining this kind of control by Japanese, collaborators, and traitors. What was effective was an angry, spontaneous stirring among the people down at the grass roots, which began without discipline and gradually evolved its own, new kind of discipline. In China as in Europe it was soon discovered by the grimmest kind of experience that in a resistance movement the previously anonymous character, known only to a few neighbors, often had a higher survival value as a leader than the well-known, widely respected man in outwitting the secret police, planted spies, informers, and traitors.

Men who began as leaders of tiny knots of resistance gradually built up their own pyramids of authority in districts and wider regions. The men at the tops of these pyramids held their power not so much by delegating authority downward to their subordinates as by accepting responsibility delegated to them upward from the grass roots. The pyramids that grew wider at the base were headed by men who never lost their contact with the grass roots. The others were discovered and demolished by the Japanese.

The growth of this kind of mixed political and military resistance movement, both in China and in Europe, evolved a rough but very vigorous democracy of its own. When resistance begins among small groups of neighbors, meeting in secret and in fear, there is apt to be a moment when everybody agrees about what should be done, but all realize the danger to the man who undertakes to get it done. At such moments, there is a kind of man to whom people turn, saying "Joe is the man to do it. We all know Joe." This kind of man who is pushed into being a hero, more than the man who romantically steps forward saying "I'll be the hero," is likely to develop into the sort of popular leader who, while acquiring greater and greater authority, never loses his democratic sensitivity to the interests of the people who have trusted him and pushed him forward. During the war, the Chinese Communists infiltrated a number of the spontaneous resistance groups and won over many of the leaders of this type, but many such groups and leaders remained quite independent of the Communists. By 1945 it was already evident that if there was going to be a civil war, it would be decided by the number of such groups and their leaders who came to terms with the Kuomintang or the Communists.

During the war, the Chinese Communists exploited an area of political thinking and method in between the Kuomintang and the grass roots. They operated simultaneously in two ways, as a broad mass movement and as a tight, disciplined party with restricted membership within the mass movement. Like the Kuomintang, the Communist Party gave its membership repeated indoctrination drills during the war, rotating members through special schools and preparing "cadres" to be pushed forward as rapidly as possible into territory recovered from the Japanese at the end of the war. Like the spontaneous grass-roots movements, and unlike the Kuomintang, the mass movement side of Communist activity recognized that its own survival would depend on popular support, and therefore provided channels through which popular support could be guided into active resistance against the Japanese.

The Communists set out to win a wider leadership by making themselves more proficient in popular leadership than the spontaneous movements. Out of guerrilla warfare and sabotage they evolved a superior type of mobile warfare capable of being co-ordinated and synchronized over wide areas through a combination of skilled staff work and the careful training of detachment leaders in the proper balance between carrying out a general directive and exercising initiative locally.

On the political side the Communists evolved a combined art and science of studying the needs of the people, evaluating the desires, hopes, and fears of each class within society, and analyzing their own resources as a party in military leadership, political propaganda, control of economic resources, and ability to organize. They steadily improved their skill in combining all these factors in such proportions as to group behind themselves the maximum possible thrust of popular approval and support, while themselves retaining control of the direction of the thrust.

Like all Communists, Mao Tze-tung and his followers believe that the impulse toward revolution may arise spontaneously, but that the success of any revolution is directly proportional to the degree that the men who are leading and directing it know what they want, and how to go about getting what they want. Stalin quotes from Lenin: "None other than Lenin said and repeated tens of times the well-known thesis that '*Without revolutionary theory there can be no revolutionary movement.*' " [1] Both the writings of Mao Tze-tung and the history of his leadership of the

---

[1] "Historicus," in the article on "Stalin on Revolution," in *Foreign Affairs* already cited above in Chapter IV; italics as in original.

Chinese Communists prove that there is no difference between his point of view and that of Stalin in this respect.

What went on in Free China, Communist China, and Occupied China during the war made inevitable a race, when Japan surrendered, to see who could take over the most territory. The surrender came at a moment when no large Chinese forces had been able to roll forward in a general offensive of their own, gaining prestige by taking back large blocks of territory. The Kuomintang and Chiang Kai-shek went into the race with their prestige damaged by the fact that in their last large-scale actions before V–J Day they had been entirely on the defensive and had been smashingly defeated by the Japanese, but with the advantage of the widely known fact that it was they who had the official support of America. The Communists, on the other hand, had stepped up the intensity of their mobile warfare in the last months of the war, and consequently went into the race for new territory with their prestige at the highest level that it had attained during the war.

As the race opened out, Chiang Kai-shek was given the further advantage of direct American help. American forces from the Pacific, landing on the coast of China, took over key points and held them for the Kuomintang, although many of these points were closer to Communist-held territory than to any Kuomintang army. Kuomintang troops were ferried to key inland and coastal points by American air lifts and naval vessels. In the meantime the Russians, in the last week of the war, had broken through into the north-eastern provinces (Manchuria). Here the Russian influence and the American influence on postwar China met.

There are several aspects of this postwar phase, preparatory to general civil war, which have never been made sufficiently clear to the American public. In the first place, while the Russians still held key cities in Manchuria, American planes and ships were pouring Kuomintang troops into Manchuria, and into North China for deployment into Manchuria. At the same time the Chinese Communists who were swarming across country into Manchuria were getting there on their own feet, not by Russian transportation.

In the second place, the Russians withdrew from Manchuria before the Americans withdrew from North China. When they withdrew, they left great stocks of captured Japanese equipment. Very few of these arms went straight into the hands of the Chinese Communists. There were at this time in Manchuria only small remnants of the old resistance movement, most of which had been crushed by the Japanese; but all over Manchuria local people picked up the surrendered Japanese arms stacked by the Russians and stood by to see what was going to happen next. It was then a question whether the Manchurian Chinese would find it easier to deal with the Kuomintang or with the Communists. When the archives are eventually opened it will be proved that all this was known in detail to American intelligence men at the time.

In the third place, where the Kuomintang got hold

of territory because of the Americans, it got it because
the Americans advanced. Where the Communists got
hold of territory because of the Russians, it was after
the Russians had withdrawn, and in part because the
Russians had withdrawn. It would be hard to exag-
gerate the psychological importance of this point in
Chinese politics.

Controversies over the policies of China's allies in
this respect link up with controversies in China's own
politics. Even before civil war gained such headway
that it had to be fought to a finish, the Kuomintang
pressed hard on its claim that territory which had been
defiled by the presence of the Japanese could only
be "restored to Chinese sovereignty" by being taken
over by accredited troops and agents of the Kuomintang. Because of the Russians and fear of what the
friends of the Russians might get away with there was
special emphasis on this doctrine in Manchuria; but
the same doctrine was asserted everywhere in China.
The fact that the Japanese had gone was not sufficient.
Nor was the fact that the people living in such territories were Chinese, who were capable of maintaining order and of electing people to represent them
before the government, or in the government.

In "China proper," south of the Great Wall, Kuomintang intransigence on this point was devastatingly
effective in turning away local resistance organizations
and pushing them into the arms of the Communists.
Wherever resistance had flourished, the people were
afraid that in a general reshuffle, with the Japanese
gone and new authorities coming in, there would be

grabbing right and left for properties that had changed hands several times during the years of Japanese occupation. They were afraid of returning landlords, who had been sitting out the war in Free China, who might want to collect rents for years back. They suspected, all too often quite rightly, that the Kuomintang cadres who were coming in to take over were fat cats, looking for cream. They felt that their only security lay in insisting on their right to go on being represented by the men who had shown themselves trustworthy leaders during the war. As soon as the Kuomintang tried to oust such men, while the Communists offered to accept them in the expanding "liberation movement" with full right to represent their villages and districts, the people tended to edge over toward the Communist side.

In Manchuria, the Kuomintang version of "restoration of sovereignty" was even more disastrous. The Manchurian Chinese had wanted to fight in 1931, when the Japanese first attacked them. The Kuomintang view at that time had been that it was too soon to fight; the northeasterners had better sweat it out until some time in the future, which turned out to be fourteen years away. Moreover the Manchurian Chinese is a kind of Chinese Texan. He is often called, by foreigners, a separatist, which he is not. His attitude is exactly like that of the Texan who considers that it would be a perversion of democracy for Washington to send anybody to Texas to mind Texas's business, while the essence of democracy is for Texas to send as many people as possible to Washington to mind the business of the other forty-seven states. Manchurian Chinese "separatism" has always demanded a combination of "State rights" and strong Manchurian representation in the national government.

The Kuomintang, during the war, showed itself an incompetent Tammany. It did not get young, enthusiastic men down from the northeast, indoctrinate and train them so that at the end of the war they could do the taking over in Manchuria. At the end of the war the Kuomintang turned up at the gates of Manchuria with a lot of carpetbaggers from the Yangtze Valley who could not even talk the local dialect properly. The northeasterners were as outraged as Texans would be if, say, they had been occupied for fourteen years by Mexico, and a Republican Administration in Washington then sent down a lot of deserving Republicans from Maine with the peremptory order that until these men took over Texas, United States sovereignty in Texas could not be regarded as restored.

The Communists, lightly armed and hiking into Manchuria by the hard overland route through Inner Mongolia, had a bad time at first against fresh Kuomintang troops with American equipment; but they had an easy time of it politically. All they had to say to the Manchurian Chinese was, "They're trying to pull the same raw stuff on you that they're trying to put over on us. How about getting together?"

Full-scale civil war was preceded by a year and a half of military and political maneuvering. Toward the end of 1945 General George C. Marshall was sent out to China, where by that time General Patrick J. Hurley had become a noisy failure as Ambassador. The frame of reference within which he was to work was indicated by a statement made by President Truman on December 15, 1945; among the things that the United States then "believed essential" were truce between the Kuomintang and the Communists and "a national conference of representatives of major political elements," to develop "a solution which will bring about the unification of China."

General Marshall failed. He was fairer than the Kuomintang was, not only to the Chinese Communists but to all minority groups which were trying to get themselves into business as political parties by lining up with the popular demand for representative government. His crippling handicaps were two. As already pointed out, it seemed to the Chinese that he did not represent a general American policy toward all countries, but an emergency policy of patching things up in China. More important still, though personally a fair and dispassionate mediator, he did not represent a neutral country. All during the period of his mission, the Kuomintang kept accumulating American supplies and American transportation kept moving Kuomintang troops into North China and Manchuria.[2]

When General Marshall gave up his mission and

[2] For a vivid description of this period by an eyewitness who covered a great deal of territory, see Richard E. Lauterbach, *Danger From the East*, New York, 1947.

returned to America to become Secretary of State he issued, in January 1947, his famous report to the President on China. In it he blamed extremists of both sides for the troubles of China, and praised a "splendid group of men" in the middle who could, if allowed, do a great deal for China.[3] Separately from this report he denied that there was any "significant aid" from Russia to the Chinese Communists, thus making it possible to handle the Russian issue separately from Chinese internal politics, though the two problems could still be combined if necessary. This Marshall policy was a statesmanlike effort to secure for the United States a position of free maneuver. It was obvious that if significant aid from the Russians began to become evident, the United States would have justification for re-entry. At the same time the Kuomintang was in effect warned that if it wanted more active American support, it should produce policies capable of winning wide popular approval in China, in order to give the United States something hopeful to support.

The first damage to this position of maneuver was inflicted by President Truman. His Truman Doctrine, proclaimed early in 1947, offered support to any country claiming to be under pressure either from Russia or from its own Communists — with no reforms stipulated and no questions asked. A year later the 80th Congress tied up in a neat package the goods first laid on the counter by President Truman. In voting funds to implement the Marshall Plan it told the Secretary of State that he would get the money for Europe

[3] For text, see Lauterbach's book, *Danger From the East.*

only after he had first trotted back to the State Department to draft a parallel plan for China — and the money for China was subtracted from the Marshall Plan for Europe. He was, to use the ugly word for it, blackmailed into destroying what remained of the position of free maneuver in China policy which he himself had set up.

All through 1947 and the first part of 1948 the Kuomintang drove ahead hard in the civil war, convinced by the general trend of American policy that they need make no concessions and that if they got into difficulties America would be forced to bail them out. The middle groups which Marshall had attempted to encourage were put out of business. Weak and pliable men were bribed or intimidated. Tougher men were killed by political gangsters, or driven into exile, or into Communist territory. Economically, the cities were plundered by black-marketeers who had Kuomintang ward boss protection. In the country, the landlords were given power to collect back rents for the war years. Peasants were conscripted into the army and for transport work.

On the military side, the Kuomintang commanders believed that if they held the "nerve center" cities and the connecting railways they could paralyze or control the nonindustrialized countryside. But modern industry has not yet been integrated with the whole economic complex to a degree that makes such a strategy possible in China. In 1947 and 1948 the Communist way of fighting a civil war began to get the upper hand. First the Kuomintang-held cities north of the Yellow River and in Manchuria were isolated. Then the railways were harried. The rural population was organized, primarily through mutual help units, in such a way that food production could be kept up and at the same time a surplus of manpower provided for military service and transportation. The Communists maintained both mobile "professional" armies and home-guard militia units. Redistribution of land convinced the peasants that both in the army and in the militia their sons were fighting to protect their own property by preventing the return of the landlords and the Kuomintang. In the meantime, in Kuomintang-held territory, the peasants were disaffected and gave help to Communist raiders, because their sons were being conscripted to protect the land of the landlords, and not to defend any interest of their own.

In the last months of 1948, as the first surrounded cities in Manchuria fell, the Communists won from the surrendering Kuomintang troops the weapons that were to prove decisive: light, mobile American artillery. The Kuomintang, shutting itself up in cities, had immobilized this artillery. The Communists, exploiting mobility to the full, won a military superiority that grew more and more devastating. In the wholesale surrenders of Mukden and Chinchow alone, the Communists captured American equipment valued at more than the $125,000,000 of the 1948 program of military aid to Chiang Kai-shek. By the end of the year they were blasting their way into cities and drawing circles of fire around Kuomintang armies in the field that were attempting to withdraw from city to city. The surrender of complete Kuomintang armies, in pockets, became commonplace. At the same time, industrial workers in cities such as Tsinan began to become important: occupying and defending their factories, they foiled the Kuomintang scorched-earth policy of destroying industry in a city that could be held no longer.

By 1949, there was a new and different China, confronting American policy with baffling problems. Clearly, the Communist ascendancy had become so decisive that it could not be reversed. Clearly, the Kuomintang had not been defeated for lack of aid. It had had the use of an unchallenged air force, provided and trained by America. It had had an American-provided naval force to control the coast. It had started the civil war with some thirty modern, American-equipped divisions, many of them American-trained. Defeat had been largely due to the demonstrated inability of the high command to use the lavish American aid provided. It had also been largely due to lack of morale among the troops. American-trained troops surrendered with the same alacrity as raw provincial levies, the moment they had the opportunity. The American artillery, which proved so effective in Communist hands, continued to be manned almost entirely by American-trained gunners. Civil and administrative disintegration matched military collapse. Kuomintang China withered on the vine not from lack of American economic aid, but from misuse of it, partly through corruption and partly through sheer incompetence.

The outcome of the war was determined not so

much by the striking power of the Communists as by the galloping process of collapse in the Kuomintang armies and government structure. As vast territories toppled into the laps of the Communists they were faced with a serious shortage of leadership, particularly of men with experience in the administration of cities. With a very small number of actual Communists in relation to the enormous total population, there was no question of converting or indoctrinating. The first problem was to administer. And the primary question was not the degree of control or dictatorship they might be able to impose but whether they would be able to give the people enough to prevent chaos.

The resulting government cannot be a "Communist government." It will have to be a coalition government, because in order to administer without chaos the Communists must deal with many groups. The outcome will be something quite different from the coalition that could have been obtained in China when General Marshall was negotiating there, and might have been obtained if military aid to the Kuomintang had been suspended. Coalition in 1946 would have meant a political coalition of non-Communists and the Communist Party, with the balance of military power on the non-Communist side. In such a coalition the parties in between the Kuomintang and the Communists, though small and weak themselves, would have been able to influence the direction followed by either the Kuomintang or the Communists.

In coalition in 1949, the non-Communists can expect to wield no more than a moderating influence.

They may be able to slow down the pace at which the Communists move, but not to change the direction in which they are moving.

In the kind of coalition that is possible in 1949 old Marshal Li Chi-sen and the "splinter groups" of liberal exiles in Hong Kong will have a limited and specialized importance. They took refuge in Hong Kong because they opposed Chiang Kai-shek but did not have the power to oppose him actively. They are therefore unable to make power bargains with the Communists. They will be primarily symbols of the fact that the Communists are not using their own power to exterminate political liberals and the educated middle classes. Some individual liberals like Sun Fo, put on the war criminal list by the Communists because they stayed with Chiang Kai-shek too long, will have great difficulty getting off the list, great difficulty getting into a coalition government, and little influence if they do get in. Although Sun Fo bears the name of his famous father, Sun Yat-sen, his political weakness is that he represents only a small clique of bureaucrats in the Legislative Yuan, which has always been intellectually pretentious but politically powerless. There is no large class, even of intellectuals, that would vote for him all over the country. He has no organization in any geographical region. Nor does he have at his disposal a body of troops.

The major elements out of which a coalition can now be built are geographical regions, armed forces, and social classes. The powerful Mohammedan lead-

ers of the provinces of Ninghsia, Chinghai, and parts
of Kansu may yet be able to make deals with the
Communists even though they have been put on the
war criminal list. The Communists are as anxious to
prove that they can get on with the Mohammedans as
they are to win support of the Mongols. Practically
every nation in Asia has important minority problems.
It is a standard operating procedure of the Communists to get the minorities on their side, as far as possible, before tackling problems of revolution among
the majorities.

Other local war lords are quite likely to be able to
strike bargains with the Communists in the western
and southwestern provinces of Szechuan, Yunnan and
Kweichow, and in many territories south of the
Yangtze. In all these provinces there is an old tradition
of keeping on good terms with the Central Government, while avoiding interference by the Central
Government as far as possible. Before the civil war
spreads into these provinces, local big shots who have
treated the people with reasonable decency realize
that they have a much better chance of negotiating
before fighting has begun than after it has started.

By far the most delicate problem for the Communists, however, is that of political coalition between social classes. Coming to power primarily
through the drive of a peasant rebellion, they now
confront both the urban middle classes and the urban
industrial workers. The middle classes accept the
Communists with trepidation, but have no will to
fight them. They are war-weary, and the Kuomintang

looted the national economy from 1945 to 1948 so thoroughly that the middle class no longer has the strength to be independent. It must either seek a foreign alliance or lean on some stronger political group in China. Many middle-class Chinese would rather work for an independent Chinese state, even if they cannot control it, than for foreign patrons who, however well-intentioned, could not help restoring the old and hated subordination of China's interests to foreign interests. They therefore fear the Russians who may be behind the Chinese Communists more than they fear the Communists themselves; but they try to comfort themselves with the assurance that the Communists will need their knowledge of business and administration.

For this they have some justification. It is imperative for the Communists, in order to consolidate their power, to give at least relative peace, order, and prosperity as a contrast to the long nightmare of the war of survival against the Japanese, followed by civil war. Throughout both the war and the civil war, they have in fact encouraged free private enterprise more than has the Kuomintang. While the Kuomintang placed politicians in positions where they could loot the industries and business enterprises to which they were attached, the Communists appear to have worked out a simple rule of thumb: they encouraged free private enterprise, both in farming and in urban production, because it was the simplest way of increasing the supply of food and commodities for the community.

As the Communists progressed from local power to

control of the national balance of power their policy-
drafting councils began to issue both invitations and
warnings. Managerial, service, and technical personnel
of all kinds were invited to stay on the job, with wages
and salaries guaranteed and with standards of living
protected by price controls. Along one important
stretch of railroad taken over in 1948 it was claimed
that 70 per cent of all employees decided to stay, including enough of the more highly paid supervisory
staff to put the line quickly back into service again.
Until the Communists took their first big cities in
Manchuria, they had never administered a municipality
with a population of more than about 100,000 population. In Manchuria they began training cadres to take
over other big cities; but they are still seriously short
of people who know how to operate city power and
light services, keep water running in the taps, and run
a bus or streetcar schedule. They know that con-
scripting such people only leads to confusion; their
shortages compel them to try to offer terms that make
life as bearable as possible for as many people as possible.

Most important of the warnings issued are those to
labor unions, against "excessive leftism." Workers are
being told that they must not strike indiscriminately,
demand get-rich-quick wages, or shorten working
hours unreasonably. Production must be kept going,
and the kind of owner who is not simply a profiteer
but is himself active in creating production must be
allowed conditions that encourage him to stay in production.

It is obvious that for people who believe in the

tenets of Marxism all such arrangements must be make-shifts, and will last only until the Communists can guide the changes they want into channels that con-form to their ideas of what human society is and how it works. As revolutionaries in practice, they have come to power through the support of peasants. As revolu-tionaries in theory, they believe that the rising class is the industrial workers; it is this class, according to their books and theories, that is destined first to win as-cendancy over all other classes and then, at some time in the future, to create a permanently classless society. They clearly aim to make their coalition government of China basically a coalition between peasants and workers, with the middle classes attached as it were at one side, in positions in which they can contribute to administration and production, but without the power to force any deviation from ultimate goals. But this aim cannot be rapidly achieved.

The crux of the problem, for the Communists, is the fact that the peasants, whom they consider the less revolutionary class, are in the ascendancy and hold the balance of armed power. They are the liberators. The industrial workers, who in Marxist terminology are the more revolutionary class, are the liberated. They are the minority both in numbers and in power. Yet Marx-ist doctrine requires that they be so placed in the coali-tion that ultimately they can hold the decisive power. In this problem lies the explosive potential that will dominate both the internal politics of China and the relations between a Communist-dominated China and a Communist-ruled Russia.

The peasants in Communist China are today the

strongest political reality, because they form more than 80 per cent of the population, and because they have private property in land and arms to defend it with. Ever since 1928 when the Communists lost the cities and retreated into the most backward rural districts Mao Tze-tung has been rising to supreme leadership by slow stages, each stage marked by bitter disputes with others who did not believe, as he did, that the Communists could survive and ultimately win domination in China by relying primarily, and at times almost exclusively, on peasant support. For the past ten years at least the primary device in expanding Communist control has been the expropriation of the land of landlords and the richest peasants, and the distribution of it to poor and "middle" peasants not as collectivized property but as private property. The result is that at the present time the center of gravity of Communist power is still in rural China, whereas in Russia by 1918–1919 it was already definitely in the cities and the factories.

During the resistance against Japan and the civil war since then the identification of the peasant with private property has been peculiarly intensified. In the fluid phases of guerrilla warfare, the Communist practice in territory which they could "liberate" only temporarily was to distribute land, then warn the peasants that the Communists could not protect their new ownership for them. Instead, they issued to the peasants as many rifles as they could spare, and moved on to other districts. The peasants then had to organize themselves by simple town meeting methods to decide who should serve in the village militia, who should cultivate the land for the men on service, and so forth. By 1949, many millions of peasants had come to feel thoroughly comfortable in a triple combination of ownership of land, experience in the use of arms to defend their ownership, and rough but workable town meeting democracy for the definition of rights, the assignment of duties, and the election of representatives.

Such a combination never developed among the peasants in Russia. Lenin used the Russian peasants to help overthrow the Tsarist state, but at the same time sidetracked them and prevented them from controlling the revolution, when he invited them to seize the land for themselves. Bolshevik organization was strongest among the industrial workers; and industry was more highly developed and widely distributed in Lenin's Russia than it is in China today. Unlike the Chinese Communists, the Bolsheviks worked outward from the cities to bring the countryside under control. Farm collectivization became possible only when the Bolsheviks had assembled enough tractor brigades to be able to send out "expeditionary forces" to plow collectivized land on behalf of the poor peasants when the rich peasants attempted to resist collectivization by limiting cultivation. From the anti-Communist point of view, the Russian Revolution was finally decided when the collective-minded industrial workers were able to crush the private-property-minded peasants. From the Communist point of view, it was decided when the industrial workers were able to "liberate" the poor peasants by crushing the rich peasants, and to

give farming a quasi-industrial character by the organization of tractor-powered collectives.

In China, on the other hand, it may be conceded
that the Communists hold the confidence of the peasants to such an extent that they can probably do more
by persuasion, with less resort to coercion, than any
previous revolutionaries in history. But the Communists cannot indulge in experiments which the peasants
do not accept, because the armed and organized peasants would be able to resist them just as they have
hitherto resisted the return of the landlords.

The Chinese Communists have developed with considerable success their own substitute for collectivization. With each family still owning its farm as private
property, labor is organized in the busiest farming sea-
sons in co-operatives which work on each farm in turn,
getting more done in a shorter time than would be possible if each family worked separately. This method
achieves about as much rationalization and technical
improvement as is possible when work is limited to
human labor and crude hand tools, with few animal-
drawn plows and practically no power-driven machines. Under such conditions collectivization of the
actual ownership of the land, merely for the sake of
Marxist orthodoxy, would bring no improvements,
because tractors and other machines are not available
to supersede the voluntary work co-operatives which
the peasants like because they bring in more grain than
the old way of working.

Revolution cannot be carried further among the
Chinese peasants until the urban workers have been

organized and made as loyal to the Communists as the peasants are, and until industrial production has been increased and improved to the point where it becomes possible to invade rural China with machines. When the Communists do take in hand the organizing of industry and the industrial workers, however, the economic center of gravity will begin to shift, and so will the political center of gravity. Long association with the peasants has opened the way to power in the higher ranks of the Communist military and political leadership for men of peasant origin. Up through these ranks there will now begin to thrust new claimants to leadership — industrial workers less experienced as Communists, but demanding rapid promotion and more authority because of the importance of the interests they represent. It can be predicted with absolute certainty that there will be changes in the top ranks of the Communist leadership, and that these changes will be accompanied by changes of policy. What cannot be predicted accurately is the rate of change.

CHAPTER VIII

CHINA, RUSSIA, AND AMERICA

ALL political theory is limited by the conditions to which it is applied. The Chinese Communists can no more behave as if China were just like Russia than the Kremlin could behave as if Russia were just like China. We must not allow speculation about other people's dogmas to distract our attention from the practical limitations that will determine just how Communist the new government in China can be and to what extent it can be dominated or influenced by Russia.

China is part of a complex situation. While the number of machines and technicians that Russia may be able to spare for China will be critical in determining China's relations with Russia, the ability of a Communist-controlled China to offer semi-processed raw materials to Japan in return for machines could stimulate in Japan a demand for the ending of American economic control. America, in turn, is the greatest potential supplier of capital, capital goods, and technicians for China; and if they can get what they need from America, it will be practical politics for the Communists to slow down their revolutionary consolidation to an evolutionary pace.

There is a tendency to assume that China's relations with Russia will be determined by the fact that the Chinese Communists are a junior Marxist party which will unquestioningly accept the decisions of Moscow. The truth is that in China devotion to nationalism and national interests is more powerful among more people than devotion to Marxism and Russian interests. Attempts by the Russians to make the Russian interest override the Chinese interest could easily bring into being a Chinese Titoism.

The rise of Titoism in Yugoslavia has shown that there can be decentralization as well as centralization in world Communism, and that the politics of repulsion, as well as of attraction, can operate between Communist states just as they do between other states. Tito was the first Communist rebel against Moscow who was able to carry with him not merely a little fragment of a party but a government and a state. China, with a population of about 450,000,000 people, is infinitely more important than Yugoslavia with its 16,000,000 people.

A Communist Party has come to power in China with even less help from Russia than in the case of Yugoslavia. To hold power, it obviously does not need to rely on the Russian Red Army. China is the only Communist-controlled country in the world with a population larger than that of Russia — about twice as large — and with a victorious army of several million men. Its top political and military leadership is not Moscow-trained. These basic facts are so important that they are capable of changing the whole internal balance and cohesion of world Communism. If the Chinese Communists gravitate toward a political center in Russia, we shall have one kind of world. If they maintain their own political center of gravity in China, we shall have a decidedly different kind of world.

It must be added that from the Russian point of view there is no urgent need to push beyond the present state of affairs in China. A China which America is unable to control is enough to safeguard Russia's continental flank in Asia. A thoroughly Communized China would give Russia no great advantage in offensive strategy against America. Russia is under no compulsion either to exhort the Chinese Communists to move quickly from coalition government to Communist dictatorship or to weaken its policy in Europe by detaching large numbers of men and quantities of material to carry out a policy of "taking over" China. On the other hand, in the many fields where there is no conflict of Chinese and Russian national interest, China will now cordially support Russia.

Russia, if it tried to take over China, would run into limitations on its power that would be different from those that baffled first Japan and then America; but the limits would be there. The Japanese, watching America's failure to control the situation in China through the Kuomintang, have been giggling in their kimono sleeves. In a queer way, it has helped to restore their self-respect. It has also given them a new respect for China, which is widely reflected in Japanese publications. The Japanese began by trying to do in China exactly what we later tried to do. They tried it after much more thorough preparation, and with a wider and deeper expert knowledge of the language, literature, history, traditions, and social and economic structure of China. They failed, and it now comforts them to see that we, with our immense weight of money and materials, have failed too.

We have forgotten, all too quickly, that before the Japanese invaded China on a large scale they tried for years to take over the Kuomintang and Chiang Kai-shek personally. They did not want to conquer China. They wanted to master-mind the Chinese government, and to train and equip Chinese armies and provide the know-how for the industrial exploitation of China, in order to build up a watertight bulkhead sealing Russia off from Eastern Asia. Only when they failed did they try the direct invasion of China as a second-best idea.

It took three years and from two to four billion dollars of American money to prove the uselessness and waste of an American attempt to imitate this early Japanese policy in China. The fault did not lie with the State Department. From the beginning Secretary Marshall and the State Department's career experts on China were convinced that China was too big, too lacking in communications and in the stiffening framework of modern forms of economic and political organization to be successfully masterminded by us. The blame for optimistically believing that the Chinese would go on acting as cannon fodder forever if we would only give them guns and call them heroes lies on the fire breathers in the 80th Congress and the tom-tom beating in the jingoistic sections of the press. Had it not been for them Secretary Marshall could have kept our interests, our strategic position, and our prestige from being so heavily involved in the collapse of the Kuomintang.

While there has been severe damage to American prestige and to the American power position, these losses cannot automatically be transposed to the other side of the ledger as Russian profits and gains. The military aspect of the situation is an example. America exercised a large measure of indirect control over the Kuomintang armies. That control was lost along with the armies which surrendered to the Communists with their American equipment intact. But this does not mean that either the Communists or the Russians standing in the background have acquired a large reservoir of trained manpower which will be blindly obedient to their commands.

For the same reasons that we could not mastermind China, the Russians will not be able to stroll in and nonchalantly take over. The present top leadership of the Chinese Communists consists of men who, however closely they may study the Moscow line and however publicly they may proclaim their loyalty to Moscow, have built their own army and their own political machine. Generals who have built their own armies and won clinching victories with them, and politicians who have built their own machines and taken over the government, are not going to turn to foreigners, even if the foreigners are their best friends, and say to them humbly, "You are so much smarter than we are; please take over!"

Apart from the question whether they can master-mind the Communists enough to give political orders, the Russians are physically incapable of exporting into China the factory output that America poured in during the last three years and more. There does not exist in Russia a two billion dollar surplus of anything that can be put into China, in the form of munitions, food, agricultural equipment, consumer goods, or anything else whatever. Nor do the Russians start out with the advantage of being the "favorite foreigners" of the Chinese, as the Americans have long been. In the Chinese folk tradition, the Russians have always been the most barbarian of the "foreign barbarians," the "dangerous neighbors" with a common frontier.

The fact is that the Russians, like the Americans, are going to find that what counts in China is the kind of government evolved by the play of Chinese political, economic, social, and military forces. We can no longer regulate the adjustment of those forces. We could not do so even by agreement between ourselves and Russia. To put it in another way, there is now virtually no limit to the ability of the Chinese to maneuver and take advantage of rivalry and hostility between us and Russia. But there are very definite limits on the ability of the Russians to exploit distrust or bad feeling between us and the government of China. There are even narrower limits on our ability to fish in troubled waters between China and Russia. Our power in China has suffered a sharp decline; but not everything that we have lost has been gained by Russia. The difference accrues to China, and the China of the next few decades will be no puppet or pushover for the Russians.

Manchuria will be the most critical test of relations between Russia and China, because in Manchuria Russia has the power to make Russian interests override Chinese interests. Manchuria has the biggest and most diversified industries in all China, and these industries are based on their own local raw materials — unlike the industries of Shanghai, which depend on raw materials brought in either by sea or down the Yangtze from the distant hinterland. Linking its industries together, Manchuria has a greater mileage of railways per hundred square miles of territory than any other group of provinces in China. In addition to everything else, Manchuria is the only industrial area in China that not only feeds itself but has a surplus of food for export.

Because of its geographical position between Japan, Korea, and Siberia, Manchuria is the only corner of China through which Russia could be invaded by American land forces with naval and air support. Such an invasion might be a major mistake in American strategy, but is a contingency which Russia will fear as long as America remains in Japan. Geographical position also makes it possible, theoretically, to detach Manchuria from the rest of China and attach it as a Chinese Soviet Republic to the Soviet Union. There are Chinese who fear that Manchuria will be lost in this way, and they will not cease to fear such a possibility unless Russian policy makes it clear that the Russian intention is to let Manchuria, long separated from the rest of China by the Japanese conquest of 1931, reintegrate itself with the home country.

Russian treaty rights in Manchuria are so conspicuous that they will serve as an infallible gauge of Russian intentions. Under agreements with China signed in 1945, just as the war was ending, the Russians secured railway, naval base, and commercial rights which restore most of the old treaty rights of Tsarist Russia — those held before 1904 and lost to Japan after the Russo-Japanese War as well as those held after 1905. These agreements are to run for thirty years, or until 1975.

Under the railway agreement the Soviet Union recovered a joint interest with China in all railways originally constructed under the old agreements with Tsarist Russia, but Russian troops can use them only "in a period of war against Japan"; and at the end of the agreement all of these rail lines are to revert to full Chinese possession without any payment to Russia. Under the Port Arthur agreement, Russia secured "joint utilization" of Port Arthur as a naval base, with the right of providing the defense for the base, and the obligation of paying for installations. In this case also the base, including any installations made by the Russians, will revert to China free of cost in 1975. Under a third agreement, Dairen was to be made a free port, under Chinese administration but with joint Chinese-Russian management, and with the Russians having the right to lease piers and warehouses. In the event of war with Japan, Russia has the right to include Dairen within the naval base area of Port Arthur. This agreement also expires in 1975. Russia enjoys one other special privilege in China: the right to priority in operating a joint Chinese-Russian air route over Sinkiang, the province adjoining the Soviet Republics of Central Asia.

The Russians could probably engineer a separatist movement in Manchuria — if they wanted to; or they could override Chinese interests by using their treaty rights in such a way as to make Manchuria a Russian protectorate in fact. If they should do so, it would probably be in order to make themselves absolutely sure against American penetration into Manchuria. The price of security, in either case, would be the abandonment of a "policy of attraction" on the doorstep of Siberia toward China and acceptance of the disadvantages of a "policy of repulsion," including the encouragement of a Chinese Titoism.

On the other hand the Russians could within a year or two, if the Communist-controlled coalition government of China looks solid enough to them, renounce the treaties. They could thus allow it to be inferred that they had demanded the treaties in 1945 partly because of their distrust of the Kuomintang government, to prevent it from granting America bases in Manchuria. Such a policy, properly timed, could have a tremendous effect throughout Asia, but is not likely until the end of the American occupation of Japan.

There is a third alternative. The Russians could let these agreements run their full course, but could during the period of the agreements use their rights so clearly to the advantage of all China, as well as the

Chinese of Manchuria, that the Chinese would be convinced of the genuineness of Russian friendship. The success of such a policy would depend largely on the ability of the Russians to supply technicians and materials to maintain steady improvement, and on their willingness to avoid every appearance of taking more wealth out of Manchuria than they put in. For Communists as well as for capitalists the rule holds that a weak country never admits that the treatment it receives from a strong country is "equal" unless it is in fact more than equal.

The fate of Manchuria is vital to China. If its surplus production is drained toward Siberia instead of being turned toward China, the Chinese Communists will have to try, as did Tito in Yugoslavia, to work out some form of compromise that will allow them to retain their Communism but at the same time rely primarily on America for trade and industrialization. Manchuria is the only part of China with an industry strong enough to take part in the industrialization of the rest of China. Even if it is allowed to turn its full industrial energy southward, Manchuria cannot build all the factories that China needs; but it could strengthen China enough to make bargaining with America much easier. In this kind of association with the rest of China Manchuria would tend to become the principal focus of an industrial or proletarian Communism pressing forward steadily to supersede the peasant-based Communism that won the civil war.

Li Li-san is the personal symbol of a potentially expanding industrially based Communism. In the early days of the Chinese Communists he ranked higher than Mao Tze-tung. He advocated attempts to take and hold cities, at whatever the cost, in order to keep industrial workers in the forefront of the movement. It was through criticism of the losses and defeats suffered in these attempts that Mao Tze-tung and his peasant-based Communism eventually assumed the lead. Li Li-san then went to Russia, from which he returned many years later with the Russian armies that entered Manchuria. He has publicly avowed that in the days when he disagreed with Mao Tze-tung he was wrong and Mao was right, but it is significant that he has operated since 1945 in the area of China that has the largest industrial population and is nearest to Russia.

West of Manchuria the deployment of Russian influence through Mongolia and Sinkiang will have a critical effect on attitudes toward Russia not only in China but throughout Asia. Along the Amur and the Ussuri, the Russians are in direct contact with a Chinese population in Manchuria. Along the Mongolian and Sinkiang frontiers, they are in contact not with Chinese but with Mongols and with various Central Asian peoples, of whom the most numerous are the Uighurs of Sinkiang.

These are weak peoples, thinly inhabiting huge territories that are strategically important and have natural resources — including oil in Sinkiang — which they themselves are not yet able to exploit. They have resisted to the best of their ability Chinese colonization of their land and Chinese efforts to absorb them by making them learn Chinese and abandon ways of life that set them apart from the Chinese. Though weak, they are as nationalistic as all other peoples in Asia. Their nationalism is still seeking effective methods of political organization, and takes competitive Communist, anti-Communist, and non-Communist forms.

In the recent past, caught between the obliterating Chinese program of colonization and cultural absorption on one side and Russian Communism on the other, they have tended more and more strongly to look toward Russia, because the Russians, though as insistent on paramount power as the Chinese, have in Siberia and Central Asia encouraged minority peoples to keep their languages and revive their cultures, and have allowed them local self-government. Now they are caught between Chinese Communists on one side and Russian Communists on the other. They themselves feel the double threat of the overriding interests of more powerful peoples, and others, throughout Asia, will react toward both China and Russia according to whether they feel that the Mongols, in Inner as well as Outer Mongolia, and the Uighurs, Kazakhs, and others in Sinkiang, are getting a fair deal or are being submerged and subordinated. Afghanistan and Tibet, in the heart of Asia, will be especially sensitive to what happens in Mongolia and Sinkiang.

The relations between America and the China which is now emerging are quite different from those between China and Russia. It is impossible for Russia, standing in contact on a land frontier, not to have a political effect on China — either as a danger or as an admired example — however small the economic interchange may be. Relations between China and America are to some extent optional. It is an advantage to America to be able to trade with China, but both countries can survive without that trade. It would be a very great advantage for China to be able to draw on America for its industrialization program; but the ending of the civil war will bring so much easing of economic distress that China can coast along for a good many years without feeling compelled to make political concessions to America for the sake of getting industrial help.

With neither country so dependent on the other that it can be forced to make concessions, future relations will have to be determined by agreements that are as acceptable to one side as they are to the other. The two chief obstacles to coming to a new understanding are the Chiang Kai-shek legend, which America helped to destroy, and the fact that America stood by while the Kuomintang ruined the private-enterprise capitalists of China.

When it became plain that Chiang Kai-shek's power was collapsing and that no amount of money or arms could succeed in making him the personal ruler of China, many Americans began to turn against him, saying that he had never been anything but a war lord with medieval ideas of politics. This attitude does no credit to us as Americans. Chiang Kai-shek was for years a true national hero in China, and a great and farsighted world statesman. He wrote the last chapter of what may be called the "old diplomacy" of China;

the fact that it ended badly is as much America's fault as his.

Chiang Kai-shek was never a dictator. He came to power through manipulating a coalition of forces, and he remained in power as long as he was able to combine more than one kind of support. Throughout this period he practiced a diplomacy that had been traditional in China for a hundred years since the Opium War: the diplomacy by which a weak power tries to play powerful rivals off against each other. He foresaw the war with Japan and its consequences. Though a stubborn man, he made possible the minimum degree of compromise and co-operation between Kuomintang and Communists without which Japan would have overrun the whole of China. In repeated crises in which the most rabidly anti-Communist of his generals virtually abandoned the resistance against Japan in their efforts to reduce the Communist area of operation, he personally maintained the front against Japan.

Chiang Kai-shek was vulnerable where any statesman practicing the old diplomacy of China was bound to be vulnerable: in maneuvering at the same time to remain paramount in China and to keep the great powers engaged in rivalry with each other, there was always the danger that he might come to owe his position in China too much to some one great power. Ever since Yuan Shih-k'ai Chinese nationalism has refused to follow any man who owed his position more to foreign support than to Chinese support.

American policy fell into this trap, and in falling dragged Chiang Kai-shek down. At the end of the war he still had the respect and trust of most Chinese; but many of his lieutenants were not respected and not trusted. There was an uneasy feeling that they had encircled Chiang and were preventing him from learning the truth about how the people felt and what they wanted — especially their dread of civil war and their demand for representative government. Chiang's closest lieutenants, in the meantime, were convinced that war between America and Russia was not far away, that it could be hastened by a civil war indirectly pitting America against Russia, and that America would not be able to withdraw from intervention. They believed that war between America and Russia would solve all their problems: America would defeat Russia, and as a by-product of the American victory the Kuomintang would win the civil war without making the slightest compromise.

When the Marshall mission failed and was followed very shortly by the Truman Doctrine of uncompromising hostility to Communism and Russia on all fronts, and then by increasing demands in Congress and a large part of the American press for "all-out aid to Chiang," the most distrusted and least respected of Chiang's lieutenants were strengthened in their encirclement of him. They claimed that their forecast was being completely proved, step by step. The trend of American policy thus destroyed what was left of Chiang's freedom of maneuver and made it impossible for him to base his leadership on the progressive wing of his own party and on the groups that stood between the Kuomintang and the Communists.

With Chiang Kai-shek defeated, there is no lesser man who can be used as an instrument of American policy. Even to seek out individual moderates in a coalition government and attempt to support them, as individuals, would defeat the aims of American policy. Such men would promptly become unable to represent a genuinely moderate point of view among their own countrymen. They would be tagged as agents of America. Everything they advocated would be suspiciously rejected as a disguised American move, detrimental to the interests of China.

Any attempt to use individuals as the spokesmen of American policy would also contribute to the horrible process by which a political secret police is built up. Hitherto American observers in China, who have been acutely conscious of secret police activities in Kuomintang China, have had nothing comparable to report from Communist China. The danger of malignant secret police development begins when, after victory, a revolutionary government feels that it has to keep watch on all kinds of people who have foreign sympathies or may be receiving foreign support. And once a man in politics is attacked as representing foreign views or interests, the police are practically challenged to dig up something on him, true, half-true, or false.

We must take our stand in China on policies, not persons. The Chinese Communists have promised many compromises. The important thing is that these promises were made not to us, but to the war-weary Chinese people. The heat is on the Chinese Communists. It is up to them to make the compromises specific, and to begin to carry them out. If they are so unsatisfactory that 450,000,000 Chinese drag their feet unenthusiastically, the Communists will be in serious trouble. To get the country going again, they desperately need 450,000,000 people who are picking up their feet briskly, not dragging them.

To meet this situation the Chinese Communists have already outlined policies of stabilization, not of stepped-up revolution. To the Chinese people, they are offering rewards for all, including owners of private enterprise, who will restore production, increase the supply of the things the nation needs, and bring down prices. To all countries — with the United States specifically mentioned — they are offering the opportunity to trade on terms of business profits for business services.

The lead for the step-by-step development of a workable American policy is clear. We are in a position to accept or refrain from accepting opportunities offered for American enterprise by a new Chinese government on straight considerations of sound business. We must not spoil our favorable position by attempting at this time to declare the conditions on which we should deal with China, especially "must not" conditions threatening the Chinese that if they do certain things we will throw a cordon around them. We must at all costs avoid the appearance of wanting to punish the Chinese people for having a government which we did not inspect and approve for them in advance. Any imputation that we wish to reserve some sort of veto power over the internal policies of the new Chinese government would solidify nationalist resentment against us.

We must also abandon the stubbornly lingering delusion that we can somehow maintain footholds by supporting rump territories or rump governments somewhere south of the Yangtze, or on the coast, or on the island of Formosa. Rumps do not make good footholds. Any diehard Chinese political or military group that tries to stay in business by combining anti-Communism with the dividing up of China's territory and sovereignty is doomed. Any such attempt will be swept away by the deep ground swell of Chinese nationalism. "Our own land, under one sovereignty; our own people, under one government," is the unifying denominator of Chinese politics today.

Ever since the end of the war there has been a gathering anger in China against that trend in American policy which is interpreted to mean that America justifies any amount of suffering in China if it contributes to the grand design of American hostility to Russia. We have already done enough to goad that rising anger. It is easier for the Chinese to accept a Communist-controlled government than it is to submit to the mutilation of their territory by the chopping off of fragments under pseudo-nationalist "legitimist" regimes that would not last a week without American support.

We shall soon have a government in China firmly established in the heart of the land and controlling practically the whole of its fringes. This government will be recognized *de jure* and *de facto* by Russia, probably to be followed very soon by the Union of India and by Pakistan. It will command increasing respect in Japan. Britain is already preparing to deal with it; if Britain should hold back, both Asia and Europe will believe that it is because American policy has superseded and subordinated British interest and British policy. The damage to Britain's power prestige and to America's moral prestige would be the greatest since the end of the war. It would make the uncontrollability of Asia stand out, and at the same time show us to be devoid of any policy except a policy of control.

The new government of China will claim China's Big Five position in the United Nations, including the right of veto. By the use of our own veto, we could delay China in moving into this position — but only by some such *reductio ad absurdum* as pretending that the island of Formosa is "China."

Nationalism is the only bedrock on which a political structure can be built in China — or anywhere in Asia — today. If we are as quick as the Russians and the Communists of Asia are to build on that bedrock, then the new political structures that are being built in China and all over Asia will incorporate many features of capitalism, private enterprise, and political democracy in their "third country" architectural design. If the Russians and the Communists continue to keep ahead of us in accepting Asia on its own terms, there will be more socialism in the superstructure.

CHAPTER IX

BEACHHEADS OF EMPIRE

THE string of countries and islands looped around the coasts of Asia, in which the United States and the imperial countries of Europe have footholds of one kind or another, all belong to the same general pattern — a patchwork of foreign investment in strategically sensitive raw materials like oil and rubber, combined with remnants of alien sovereignty or control over peoples among whom the tide of nationalism is running more and more strongly. At the same time these countries and their peoples differ from each other in so many ways that it would be foolish to attempt to apply the same policy to all of them.

Can these beachheads around Asia be used to enable American and European interests to advance once more into the mainland of Asia, or must they be regarded as embarkation beachheads from which American and European interests must try to carry out an orderly evacuation and retreat? European countries, wherever they feel that a retreat from empire has become inevitable, want to carry it out as slowly as possible and to salvage as much as they can of their old vested interests. America, with both capital and military strength to spare, is more interested in opening up opportunities for establishing new interests. The general character of European policy is to permit change only where it cannot be stopped by force. The general character of American policy is to permit and even encourage the advance toward political sovereignty of formerly subject countries, as rapidly as this can be done without disorders detrimental to investment and trade, and without the danger of sudden changes from political evolution to social revolution.

India — and the Union of India more than Pakistan — is the key area within the ruins of empire in Asia. Within it there is the maximum opportunity for co-ordinating change and stabilization.

The old Indian Empire, including both the present Union of India and Pakistan, was the keystone of the arch of empire. It was so great in geographical mass, in the bulk of its population, in its importance to British strategy and military manpower, and in its economic significance, that when the two Dominions of the Union of India and Pakistan were formed by negotiation instead of armed revolution the whole structure of world empire over subject peoples was bound to begin to slump down on its foundations.

The 400,000,000 people of the Indian Empire were all nationalistic in their demands for freedom from British rule; but they were divided among themselves by tumultuous differences of political interest and political theory, sharpened by social and economic conflicts and by differences of language, culture, and religion. There was a fantastic range of economic variation. At one end the Tata steel mills were bigger than anything in Britain itself. At the other end were farmers more miserable than the poorest peasants in China, and hereditary professional beggars with a vested interest in their own running sores. In between was every imaginable degree of poverty and wealth, and every imaginable way of making a living or dragging out an existence.

The apologists of empire advertised the internal conflicts in India and drew on endless variations of the theory of trusteeship. For purposes of political justification, anything good in India could be attributed to the wisdom and benevolence of British rule. Anything bad could be cited as a warning of the horrors that would engulf India if British rule were withdrawn. It could be argued — and was argued for decades, while modern Indian nationalism was maturing and pressing its demands more and more strongly — that only a continuation of British rule in the spirit of trusteeship would slowly bring India as a whole up to the level vaguely described as "political responsibility." India was even the oldest justification for policies of defense against the Russian menace. More than half a century before the Bolshevik Revolution, apologists of British rule in India began to call the world to witness that if British rule were withdrawn from India it would only be succeeded by Russian rule.

The theory of empire as well as the structure of empire slumped on its foundations when, in the end, the British negotiated dominion status because they no longer had the power to maintain their rule by force.

It was clear that they were not suddenly convinced that the Indians had attained the vague standard of "political responsibility." The final jolt was open revolt in the Indian Army, as Prime Minister Attlee admitted in Parliament. Nothing could have been less like the staid old concept of "political responsibility." In the whole process the initiative came from the Indian side. Dominion status was not the ideal at which the British aimed but the best compromise they were able to salvage out of a situation that they were no longer able to control. Under these conditions the British carried out brilliantly a most difficult maneuver in statesmanship: the avoidance of loss of prestige when making a far-reaching concession of power.

Dominion status emerged in a whirlpool at the point where the vigorous current of nationalism meets the weakening current of imperial power. The fact that Pakistan separated from India on the issue of religious politics reveals one of the effects of British rule that nationalism has not yet been able to submerge. Encouragement of political organization within the framework of religion had, after the First World War, become the principal British device for splitting the onslaught of a united nationalism. British official and semiofficial literature persisted in referring to a supposed Hindu Congress long after the All-India Congress had made it a major policy to stress the union in nationalism of people of different religious faiths. Mohammed Ali Jinnah developed the momentum of his political career by turning this British policy to his own advantage, and he had enough momentum left, when the British withdrew, to carry out the separation of Pakistan as a personal triumph.

The new current of nationalism will eventually smooth out this whirlpool. The most statesmanlike achievement of the Union of India is its increasingly successful insistence on modern secular politics instead of the archaic politics of religion. In the case of the State of Hyderabad it succeeded in maintaining, in the face of both Britain and Pakistan, that the issue was between a despotic Nizam, as such, and his unwilling subjects, as such, and not between a Moslem ruler and his Hindu subjects. In the case of Kashmir the core of the Union of India policy, in its conflict with Pakistan policy, has been its insistence on the right of a Moslem leader of Kashmir to bring his Moslem followers into the multi-religious Union of India instead of into Moslem Pakistan. Eventually, this trend toward secular politics will lead to the reintegration of Pakistan and the Union of India as one federalized, multi-religious state.

In the meantime, the Dominions of India and Pakistan are changing the character of the British Commonwealth as well as the British Empire. In the dual British system the Empire is composed of subject possessions, while the Commonwealth is a free alliance. In this free alliance the European populations of Britain, Canada, Australia, New Zealand, and the Union of South Africa are now outnumbered by the peoples of India and Pakistan, whose Asian bias will have an increasing effect on British policies as a whole.

The British interest is to maintain what is left of the

system of empire for as long as possible, both in Britain's own possessions, such as Malaya, and in the possessions of Britain's allies, such as Indo-China and Indonesia and the British, Belgian, and French possessions in Africa. The interest of India and Pakistan is to eliminate what is left of the imperial system as fast as possible; and this interest leads the policies of India and Pakistan not only into Indonesia but into the Arab states and Africa. The effect of this new bias within the Commonwealth can already be seen in the case of Australia, which lies on the far side of Asia, looks toward Asia for markets for its industries, and has been more openly and consistently friendly to nationalists in Asia than either Britain or America.

The Union of India, more than Pakistan, whose freedom of maneuver is cramped by the restrictions of religious politics, is eager to build a new structure of hegemony out of the ruins of empire in Asia. As long as no nation in Asia can stand forward in world politics as a great power, all nations in Asia must either associate their interests or become in some degree the satellites of either Russia or America. If there is to be an Asian group aiming at the maximum freedom from control by both Russia and the European-American bloc, China cannot be the pivot of it because Communism is clearly in the ascendant in the Chinese coalition. Such an association can only work and represent common interests if the emphasis is non-Communist rather than pro-Communist or anti-Communist. The lead therefore can be taken by India. It is for this reason that Nehru so steadily insists that the Union of India is neutral in the contending expansion of Russian and American power, and would continue to be neutral if war broke out. Pursuing this line of policy Nehru proposed, in the Asian Conference on Indonesia at New Delhi in January 1949, that the Asian nations should not act as an anti-European bloc — which would further weaken the United Nations — but should work to strengthen the authority of the United Nations Security Council.

For India and the nations that Nehru would like to group around India have more than one interest in common. Even nationalist movements that are afraid of Communism do not want to be made into the cannon fodder of an American victory over Russia. Even movements that are tinged with Communism want to win their own victories over what remains of imperialism more than they want to be sacrificed to a Russian victory over America. Conversely, both movements that are afraid of Communism and movements that are tinged with Communism have learned how to play off the American fear of Russia against the Russian fear of America to their own advantage.

Both in geographical position and in political structure the Union of India has advantages which may make it an area of stabilization in Asia; and if stabilization can be achieved in Asia, it may contribute to stabilization of the relations between Asia, Europe, America, and Russia.

The Union of India and Pakistan both resemble China in the short period when the Kuomintang was at the peak of its power, from 1928 when the Chinese

Communists were driven into the wilderness to 1931 when China began to lose territory to Japanese aggression. Both countries, however, intend to improve on the history of Kuomintang China, not to recapitulate it. They are not fooling themselves about Communism, but they realize that Chiang Kai-shek's fanatic insistence on continuing the civil war against the Chinese Communists even when Manchuria was invaded in 1931 almost made possible the complete conquest of China by Japan. Both countries, therefore, are trying to find ways to limit the activities of Communists without being led into armed crusades against Communism.

Pakistan resembles the landlord-dominated hinterland of rural China in the days of Kuomintang power. The Moslem combination of authoritarianism within the political movement, the profession of brotherhood among all who are of the faith, and harsh insistence on conformity reads like a religious version of right-wing Kuomintang principles of organization.

The Union of India resembles the full Kuomintang coalition of 1928 between landlords and modern capitalists. The key position is held by the modern capitalists, whose political representative is Sirdar Vallabhbhai Patel, not Nehru. Their drive toward nationalist independence was motivated by the fact that under British rule British capitalism in India was bound to be stronger than Indian capitalism. Under Indian rule, they do not object to the activity of either British or American capital, because they need more capital to promote their own interests, and can control the conditions under which capital operates.

The fact that nationalism has already won for them so much of what they want makes them insist that revolution in India has now gone far enough. From now on, the demands of urban workers, peasants, and the large and poorly paid lower middle class should be met by gradual reforms. Yet while they have safeguarded their position in India, the Indian capitalists are still weak capitalists in a world of strong capitalists. They feel that their future will be threatened if powerful combinations of European and American capital establish themselves too strongly elsewhere in Asia in control of subject populations. For this reason they are willing to keep Indian anti-imperialism alive, and to direct it against the salvaging of the old order of empire anywhere in what remains of colonial Asia. On the other hand, as capitalists themselves, they do not want to see colonial revolution become completely anti-capitalist.

These characteristics, when all put together in one bundle, make the capitalists who control the balance of power in India believe that foreign capital should not have political control in any country in Asia. They also believe, however, that the capitalists within each independent country in Asia should have as much power as possible, and should be free to negotiate for the use of as much outside capital as they need.

Although there are extremes of difference between many of the countries east and west of India, many of these differences can be accounted for by the fact that they are in different stages of the development of nationalism. Because nationalism is at work in all of them, there are in fact possibilities of stabilization based on the attainment of a less complete political independence or freedom from indirect control than each country wants, but a more complete relinquishment of rule or control than Europe or America wants. A survey, country by country, will show what facts the policy makers must accept as hard facts, and what facts are amenable to compromise.

The Philippines was the only country taken by the Japanese during the war in which the former rulers did not lose both power and prestige. The principal reason for Filipino loyalty to the United States was the fact that the Filipinos were the only dependent or subject people who had been promised complete political independence at a definite date. In all the colonial possessions of Europe, references to the future had always avoided the word "independence." Words with more than one meaning, like "self-government," were used instead and European governments never pinned themselves down to dates, but talked only of vague qualifications like "maturity" which might within unspecified periods of time qualify their subjects to ask for something less than independence.

It is true that what really determined the United States to promise Philippine independence was not the conviction that the Filipinos should be allowed to govern themselves. It was the fact that special interests in the United States which wanted the Philippines outside the tariff barrier were more powerful than special interests that wanted them within. But the fact that the United States earned great political dividends in the Philippines and throughout Asia by an accident of selfishness instead of by clear-sighted statesmanship should not detract from the value of the example when the problems of other dependent and subject peoples are considered.

Japanese occupation did result in a new kind of politics in the Philippines, however. Among the bravest guerrilla fighters against the Japanese were poor tenant farmers. Among the most pliant collaborators of the Japanese were many of the rich landlords of these farmers. Inevitably, organized political antagonism to landlords who lived in big cities under Japanese protection was a by-product of guerrilla resistance which carried over into postwar politics. Inevitably, too, this peasant radicalism was infiltrated by Communist organizers.

Postwar politics in the Philippines, because of this development and because of political independence, beginning in 1946, is three-cornered. At one corner are men who were big shots under American rule, continued to be big shots under Japanese rule, and when General MacArthur proclaimed "I have returned" echoed him with a fervent "Me too." They have developed political reflexes that respond more sensitively to the interests of a strong outside protector than to the votes of popular majorities. At another corner stand radical peasants who have had experience in armed rebellion and political organization and are now backed by a growing labor interest. At the third corner stand business and professional men who feel that they

can only organize free enterprise if they can take political control away from the old big shots whose principal skill is in rotating from one outside protector to
another, and who represent a capitalism of captive
enterprise rather than of free enterprise.

In this three-cornered politics it was a smart move
at the time but a move damaging to American interests
in the long run when General MacArthur encouraged
the election, as the first president of the free Philippines, of Manuel Roxas, who had collaborated with
the Japanese during the war (while also sending intelligence out to MacArthur), and was conspicuously a
man of the captive enterprise big-shot class. It was a
poor move because an alliance between the other two
corners will eventually dominate the triangle of Philippine politics. Captive enterprise vested interests obstruct the growth of a free enterprise capitalism, and
for this reason the Filipinos who want a free enterprise
capitalism will ally themselves, however cautiously,
with the tenant farmers who, though Communist-led,
want to own their farms as private property.

The Philippine Trade Act (Bell-Tydings Act) of
1946 shows the fundamental opposition between free
enterprise and captive enterprise in any country in
Asia that is struggling to get on its feet. The passage
of this act did shocking damage to the long-term
interests of America in Asia, and to the whole American policy of encouraging and increasing world-wide
trade. As described with cool objectivity by William
L. Clayton, then Assistant Secretary of State, in his
testimony before Congress, it gives American citizens

— "special rights we cannot give Philippine citizens."
It ties the hands of the Philippine government in the
control of Philippine products, and "not only does
this deprive the Philippine government of a sovereign
prerogative," but "new Philippine producers would
not — during the life of the Act — be able to compete
freely in their own country." The captive enterprise
interests represented by Roxas, which forced through
Philippine acceptance of this disabling Act, naturally
branded themselves in Filipino eyes as unpatriotic,
while everywhere else in Asia the Act was taken as a
warning that there may be deadly pitfalls in the path
of a country whose government seeks the approval
of the American government.

From the American point of view the Philippines,
with its new postwar politics, is partly but by no means
entirely out of control. It is under control to the extent that America can hold air, naval, and army bases
in the Philippines indefinitely, if need be. It is out of
control to the extent that it is closely linked in political
sympathy with the European colonial possessions that
are slipping out of control, and is not a good base from
which to bring them back under control. American
pressure and the use of American money in Philippine
politics will grow rapidly less effective as the years
pass; but a national hostility to America will develop
only if there is American insistence on subordinating
the Philippines to the recovery of a strong Japan.
There can hardly be, in fact, a sound American policy
for the Philippines alone; American policy toward the
Philippines will be sound or unsound according to the

part that it plays in the much larger complex policy of America in Asia as a whole.

Indo-China is the most weakly held of all colonial possessions. It was never linked with the really vital economic processes of France, as India was linked with Britain. It was, rather, a distant possession where men with the right political connections could get rich in a few years; it was probably the most corruptly administered large colonial possession in the world. During the war, the Frenchmen who controlled Indo-China under Japanese supervision were loyal to Vichy, not to France; and in France itself men whose wealth came from Indo-China through crooked channels stood close around Marshal Pétain.

Viet Namese, not Frenchmen, organized guerilla resistance in Indo-China, and it was through their underground that Frenchmen who wished to join the Free French forces escaped across the frontier into China. After the war, the French could not even have got back into Indo-China had the British not landed first and held the ports for them. By 1949, the Viet Nam nationalist movement had won control of three quarters of the country, and there was so little popular support in France for a war of reconquest that German and African troops had to be used in large numbers. With 100,000 troops in Indo-China, the French are estimated to be spending on an unsuccessful colonial war the equivalent of a third of what France itself is getting in Marshall Plan aid.

Viet Nam nationalism is led by Ho Chi Minh, a veteran Communist educated in France who later studied in Russia and worked closely with the Chinese Communists in the 1920's. There are so few Communists in Indo-China that he has not even attempted to send out a Communist spearhead in advance of the main nationalist column. He sticks close to nationalism and nationalist issues, and as a result his movement has solid support even among the upper classes living away from the French-held cities, and among Catholics. All French efforts to split up the nationalist movement by isolating the Communists have failed; there are not enough Communists to isolate. French efforts to set up local governments of pseudo-nationalists have also failed; the French cannot attempt to regain control and at the same time offer their puppets anything that looks like nationalism in comparison with the movement led by Ho Chi Minh.

The hardest of hard facts in Indo-China is that the country will become independent. American and British correspondents of the Associated Press, the *Christian Science Monitor*, and the *Manchester Guardian* were reporting before the end of 1948 that the French situation was hopeless. Reconquest of Indo-China cannot be made a national cause in France, and for America the diversion of military forces needed to reconquer the country for France would be a military absurdity and a political impossibility.

Siam is a country with no serious revolutionary movement. It is one of the few countries in Asia with a surplus of food and room for the population to expand. In the age of imperialism it remained the only independent country in Southeast Asia. Although foreign — especially British — economic interests are powerful, political independence satisfies the rather small group of families who dominate the government and army. In Latin American style, revolution has hitherto meant the ousting of one clique of families by another. Siam is a country in which a farsighted American and European policy could bring rapid progress and an all-round increase of wealth, rather than the transfer of wealth from the rich to the poor. There is one limitation: the Western countries would have to reconcile themselves — as they have never yet done in any country in Asia, except the Philippines — to the fact that education is necessary to progress and that education, alone, makes inevitable a political revolution in which the growing number of educated people demand a share of the power previously monopolized by a few rich families.

Malaya is Britain's last treasure-house colony in Asia. With a minimum expenditure on military forces, public services, and education it produced tin and rubber which are tremendous dollar-earners for Britain and in the past have enabled Britain to dominate the international cartels setting the world prices of tin and rubber.

Malaya when the British came was divided into little tribal states of Malays, each ruled by its own sultan. The British confirmed the rather grandiloquent titles of these chiefs. They "federated" some of the states

and administered them directly; others were controlled
indirectly as unfederated states. The Malays had an
easy enough life to enable them to refuse to work
as cheap plantation or mining labor. The British therefore imported first Chinese and then Indians, and the
population now consists of about 40 per cent Chinese,
40 per cent Malays, and nearly 20 per cent Indians,
with Europeans forming only a fractional percentage.

Among the industrious Chinese especially a few
poor coolies founded millionaire families owning
mines, plantations, big businesses, and banks; but they
remained colonial subjects, without a vote. (To this
day British passports distinguish between a "subject"
and a "citizen.") The Chinese, forming the bulk of the
colonial middle class and controlling the most militant
trade-unions, have taken the lead in colonial nationalism. They are divided into a declining majority organized by the Kuomintang, which wants a domi-
nating position for the Chinese with separate political
organizations for each colonial people, and a growing
minority sympathetic to the Chinese Communists, with
many Communist leaders and organizers, who want
a multinational Malayan state in which Chinese, Malays, and Indians will all be members of the same
political organizations and trade-unions.

The British, since the war, have countered by favoring a separate nationalism of the Malays, tinged with
animosity against the "intruding Chinese." Singapore
has been set aside from the rest of Malaya as a Crown
Colony, thus maintaining the disfranchisement of the
majority of the Chinese, whose center of gravity is in

Singapore. To a large extent the British have succeeded in preventing alliances between Malays and Chinese and splitting alliances between Indians and Chinese. They have also worked hard on the cleavages between middle class and labor union Chinese leadership.

Early in 1948 conferences of Indian Communists, New Democratic Youth Leagues, and Southeast Asian Students were held in Calcutta, at which Russians were present — not secretly, but "on diplomatic passports" — and after these conferences there were Communist and Communist-led uprisings in Burma in April, in Malaya in June, and in Indonesia in September.[1] It is easy to assume that the conferences were used to relay the voice of Moscow, and that the risings were Moscow-ordered. There is a supplementary explanation which points to an even more serious problem for European and American policy makers. Communist and near-Communist leaders in Asia today are much more than mere agitators. They are mature political operators, who know that their rulers consult each other and co-ordinate the timing of their moves whenever possible, and that it is essential for them to do the same thing. Some have learned, and others are learning, to listen to the Moscow radio more as a central source of intelligence on the world situation in which their local situations are involved than as a source of orders for immediate action.

As this tendency increases the Communist movements in Southeast Asia will become more formidable.

[1] Ian Morrison, "The Communist Uprising in Malay," *Far Eastern Survey*, New York, December 22, 1948.

The record shows that the Chinese Communists lost ground when they rigidly followed analyses made in distant Moscow and began to prosper when, under Mao Tze-tung, they developed a dual technique of co-ordinated timing with Moscow, as far as possible, while basing themselves primarily, within China, on their own knowledge of Chinese conditions. Similarly the success of Ho Chi Minh in Indo-China is clearly the result of his policy of not getting too far out ahead of the kind of support that an intelligent nationalist leader can mobilize in Indo-China.

The Southeast Asian risings of 1948 probably failed both because the Moscow representatives who attended the preceding conferences were too optimistic in their estimate of the weakness of the European countries and because the Southeast Asian Communists were too optimistic about the local strength that they could muster. Certainly in Malaya the local leaders got far out ahead of the line on which their non-Communist supporters were ready to stand and fight. The result, in Malaya, was that the British were able to isolate the hard core of Communism in a few Chinese-led unions and to deal with it within the dimensions of using troops against labor violence, preventing it from spreading into a nationalist rising.

The British counterattack, however, has failed. Veteran Communists with previous guerrilla experience against the Japanese have faded back into the jungles, and may be able to survive there against the British as they did against the Japanese. Whether they will be able, in the jungles, to recruit Malay followers as well as Chinese, to work back into contact with the labor unions, and to integrate the joint Malay-Chinese-Indian colonial nationalism that has always been their long-range aim will depend not simply on British military strength in Malaya but on the position of Malaya in the whole wide sweep of colonial unrest, and also on the stability in Europe itself of the Western Union group of European colonial powers.

Burma is unique in Asia in its combination of three characteristics: its European rulers admitted promptly and without fighting that they could not reconquer the country, and negotiated the recognition of full independence; it had no powerful ruling class of its own with secondary experience of government under the British; and no important political movement has emerged that is anti-Marxist or even non-Marxist in its views and aims. Burma was not oppressively ruled by the British. Why should its politicians, turning their backs on the Anglo-Saxon tradition, take Marx as their guide to the future?

The answer should be studied carefully in Europe and America. Peoples who even when ruled benevolently have been starved of political experience want to adopt at once what they consider the most modern political forms. In Asia today, that gives Marxism a head start. People in Asia who have the tradition of being a ruling class, or great wealth, or other strong vested interests are afraid of the subversive aspects of Marxism. Others, including educated people and members of the middle classes who make their living by their brains rather than by the ownership of property, are not alarmed by the fact that Marxism is subversive of the old European order. They have no loyalty to the old European order. They have no emotional attachment to European democracy, which, from their point of view, is selfishly democratic within Europe and has never exported itself to Asia. They want to strengthen themselves against and in competition with the European tradition.

If Marxism is weakening and in some countries supplanting the old European order, that makes it, from their point of view, modern and progressive. In addition, they live in countries in which the whole population can only move forward if mass support is mobilized for material progress. They will never get education, engineering, and improved farming if they simply sit and wait for them. They must be taught to want these things even before they have them. Marxist organization provides excellent techniques for these purposes. Its emphasis on innumerable councils, committees, shock brigades for emergency jobs, and so forth, provides both training at the grass roots in discussion, voting, and self-government, and a chain of command through which political directives decided on at the top can be passed back down to the grass roots, accompanied at each step by another series of councils, committees, and mass meetings at which the decisions are explained, the people are exhorted to carry them out, and committees are appointed or elected to see that they get carried out.

Burma is the purest example, because of the absence

of non-Marxist or anti-Marxist competition, of this tendency to emphasize Marxism as modern and progressive; but the same tendency is present in every country in Asia. The inclination to call Marxism progressive, and the increasing tendency to take the word "democratic" away from Europe and America and give it to Russia and Marxism are among the hard facts of the Asia of today. To try to deal with them by showing that Europe and America have enough police and military strength to resist Marxist subversion cannot be anything better than an emergency expedient. In the long run, Europe and America must be able to demonstrate that there can be progress and democracy — democracy for Asia, in forms acceptable to Asia — without Marxism.

In Burma there is more Marxist thinking than there is Marxist experience, or political experience of any kind. Consequently there is extreme confusion, with all kinds of groups, calling themselves Marxist, making and breaking alliances with each other. Personal leadership and the ability to attract personal followers are of primary importance in the formation of parties. The rivalry of parties is complicated by the fact that Burma, like so many countries in Asia, is multinational. The "hill tribes," of which politically the Karens are the most important, because of their strength in the army, can easily be organized to demand autonomy under their own chiefs. The British have been accused of working through the Karens to keep a foothold in Burmese politics. The eventual stabilization of Burma, however, may come about through its relations with

India and China rather than through the recovery of the British influence.

Indonesia, once considered the model European colony in Asia, now shares with Indo-China a reputation for devotion to freedom. The "model" rule of the Dutch — after a period of severe exploitation in the nineteenth century — stressed the leasing of land, instead of allowing purchases that would leave the Indonesians landless, and the limiting of education to prevent too many "natives" from acquiring ideas inappropriate to their station. The unexpected result, after the war, was the proof that under modern colonial conditions it takes only a handful of men with modern education to organize and lead effectively a strong nationalist movement.

Partly because Holland itself was able to stay out of the First World War, investments in Holland acquired a reputation for immunity in times of trouble, just as investments in Switzerland. These investments spread into Dutch undertakings in Indonesia, and in addition there were many direct international investments in Indonesia, whose most important products are commodities of international exchange like tin, rubber, oil, tea, kapok, quinine, and, more recently, bauxite. The Dutch now count on the sensitiveness of American and other investors to put on pressure in Washington to prevent effective action against the Dutch attempt to reconquer Indonesia.

Because Holland itself is a small and weak country, and because of the importance of international investments, Holland became an elephant-boy country, with Indonesia as its elephant. An elephant boy is a youngster who excites admiration by his calm authority over a mountainous pachyderm. He gives orders, and prods the beast with an iron hook, and the elephant obediently moves huge teak logs around. This apparent authority of the boy, however, is in reality a subsidiary phenomenon of a complex system which has come to be accepted by the boy himself, the elephant, and everybody else concerned. As long as all the elephants are working serenely, a boy is enough. Once there is trouble in the elephant herd, however, the authority of one boy over one elephant vanishes, and others have to step in.

Elephant trouble began when the Japanese invaded Indonesia. The feebleness of the Dutch resistance destroyed their prestige forever; and there was no loyalty among the Indonesians — and no reason for loyalty — to make them fight along with the Dutch as the Filipinos fought along with the Americans. The very limited self-government that the Japanese gave the Indonesians was more than the Dutch had given them, and enough to give them a little training in administration and military organization. When the Japanese surrendered the Indonesians were able not only to claim independence but to show a military cohesion and an administrative ability that astonished Americans and dismayed the Dutch.

The elephant boy was unable to climb back on the elephant without British help. A British force found that the Indonesians fought so effectively that Japanese

who had surrendered had to be armed again and sent
into battle against them: the British were unable to reconquer the islands, but they were able to get the
Dutch back in. Since then, the story of Indonesian
politics has been the story of how the Dutch have
slowly built up their military forces, winning time to
do so by setting up as many patronized and protected
states as possible to compete with the Indonesian Republic, and by resorting intermittently to sudden but
not sustained military action in order to break the organized military forces of the Republic without running the risk of a long and exhausting colonial war.

On the Indonesian side, nationalism has remained
pervasive; but Indonesia is a complex country of many
islands, stretching over a distance greater than the
distance from San Francisco to New York, and among
its diverse peoples and local interests there have been
varying degrees of willingness to fight for different
aspects of nationalism. In view of the complexity of
Indonesia, the orderliness of political growth has been
amazing. No revolutionary strong man has emerged
with dictatorial power. Except for the brief inter-
lude of the Communist rising in 1948, differences have
been adjusted by the committee method. In the sense
of the word which Americans and Europeans are most
ready to accept, the Indonesian nationalist movement
has been the most democratic of the colonial revolutions; and the Dutch therefore dealt a specially deadly
blow to Western democratic interests when they
proved that the Indonesians could not win freedom
by democratic reasonableness, but must be prepared to

match revolutionary extremism against imperialist extremism.

In 1946 the British mediated between the Dutch and the Indonesians with partial success. In 1947 Britain and America granted "limited *de facto*" recognition to the Republic, and the United States urged the Republic to co-operate with the Dutch in forming an interim federal government of territories held by the Republic and by the Dutch, "further stating that the United States was prepared to consider granting financial aid to such an interim government upon its establishment." [2] Less than a month later the Dutch went into "police action" against the Republic with tanks, planes, and amphibious operations. This resort to violence brought a United Nations cease-fire order and, a little later, the sending of a Good Offices Committee consisting of a Belgian and an Australian delegate, under an American chairman. Negotiations through this committee continued until December 1948, when the Dutch once more resorted to military action which this time, they hoped, would be conclusive.

The significance of the protracted negotiations lies in the fact that they were an appeal to reasonableness. In each crisis the pressure on the Indonesians to be reasonable was a little stronger than the pressure on the Dutch. The Indonesians repeatedly yielded a little more than the Dutch, hoping that they would gain,

[2] Raymond Kennedy and Paul M. Kattenburg, *Indonesia in Crisis*, Foreign Policy Reports, New York, December 15, 1948.

in the form of international approval, what they lost by
direct concessions. The Dutch resorted to sudden military action each time that they thought they could get
away with it — and each time they did get away with
it.

During the long negotiations there was one out-
break of violence on the Republican side — but not
against the Dutch. In September 1948 there was a
Communist rising against the Republic, led by Muso,
an old political exile who had just returned after many
years in Moscow, and Alimin, another exile, who had
lived not only in Moscow but among the Chinese Communists. They were joined by Sjarifoeddin, a founder
and former Premier of the Republic, who suddenly
declared that he had for many years been a secret
Communist.

The call to revolt accused the moderate leaders of
the Republic of being too soft, and of allowing the
Dutch to make successive encroachments that would
eventually enable them to overthrow the Republic.
Though accused of being soft toward the Dutch, the
Republic acted toughly and swiftly against the Communists, dispersing them and killing Muso and Alimin.
Then, in ironic justification of the Communist protest, the Dutch not only attacked the Republic but
accused it of being controlled by Communists.

A new colonial war is now in full blaze. The Dutch
hope to crush it because they have 125,000 highly mobile troops with excellent equipment. Their morale is
much higher than that of the French, Germans, and
Africans in Indo-China. They are good, clean Dutch

boys whose behavior in Indonesian villages has on the whole been well disciplined. They are well indoctrinated with the belief that they are saving the Indonesians from the unspeakable horrors of Communism, and do not believe that there is such a thing as a democratic but anti-Dutch nationalism. The Dutch, by sea and air observation, may be able to hamper the movement of the nationalists between islands; and on Java, the heart of the Republican movement, guerrillas will have difficulty in finding terrain where they can both hide easily and move freely.

The Indonesians, however, will probably win. There is a general and rapidly increasing sympathy for them even in the little separate states set up by the Dutch and nominally subservient to the Dutch. The moderate leaders of the Republic were captured by the Dutch and this, together with the fact that the Republican regular forces were scattered by the Dutch onslaught, will throw leadership into the hands of two very different groups — the most fanatical Moslems, and the surviving Communist leaders. Modern communications between revolutionaries in Asia are so good that the Communist leaders will soon have at their service all the fighting and organizing experience of the Chinese Communists and the Viet Nam nationalists.

Most important of all, the elephant-boy weakness of the Dutch will be exposed. For Holland, with about 9,000,000 people, the effort required to maintain a fully equipped army of 125,000 in Indonesia under the attrition of guerrilla warfare is roughly equivalent to the strain that America would feel in keeping an army of more than 2,000,000 in the field in China. Holland cannot live on its own resources, and under conditions of guerrilla warfare cannot get out of Indonesia the revenue that is needed to finance the reconquest of Indonesia. The job is too big for an elephant boy.

What the Dutch have done is to bring on a fresh crisis that will affect the whole of Southeast Asia and force America, as the subsidizer of Holland, Britain, and France, to call for a reconsideration of the colonial problem as a whole. This reconsideration will have to be carried out in an Asia which has on one flank of the colonial area a Communist-led China which has just demonstrated that it cannot be controlled by America, and on the other an India in which Nehru has called for joint action against European military intervention against subject peoples anywhere in Asia. The Asian Conference on Indonesia has shown that the European empires, even with American support, can no longer insist that their colonial interests be kept separate from the interests of Asia as a whole.

Ceylon, smaller than Ireland, is of minor importance in Asia. It has Dominion status, negotiated since the war, but is controlled primarily by plantation interests, the most important of which are British-owned.

Afghanistan in the nineteenth century lay beyond the line of diminishing returns of British expansion on the northwest frontier of India. The expensiveness of campaigning on this frontier and the poor economic returns of conquest constrained the British to limit the amount of territory annexed. Afghanistan has since been regarded as primarily a territory that ought not to be occupied by Russia. Since Afghanistan is the neighbor of Pakistan, and neither of them makes as good a base for attack against Russia as Turkey or Iran, there is at present no reason why Russian policy should be especially active in either country. Russia's primary interests lie at the western and eastern ends of the long land frontier, and would be harmed by a diversion of strength to the middle of the frontier.

Iran, once divided into spheres of interest between Britain and Tsarist Russia, is now a field of British and American interest in the south and of Soviet interest in the north. Each of these spheres of interest has its own belt of oil-bearing lands. Those in the south are worked by British and American interests; those in the north, on which Russia has options, are not being worked because American influence at Teheran is strong enough to encourage the government to refuse to allow the Russians to go ahead with exploration and development.

This stalemate is a temporary phase of the cold war. The northern oil fields, which lie on the edge of Soviet territory, certainly cannot be worked by American or British interests. As long as it remains an accepted international principle that oil lands in countries which cannot work them themselves may be exploited by outside interests, it will be impossible to maintain per-

manently the supplementary principle that only capitalist countries may exploit the oil of their weak neighbors. The political effects of such a doctrine would be
too damaging to the interests of the capitalist countries
themselves.

The Arab states were formerly in the main British
protectorates, with French interests in Syria and Leba-
non. The original British interest was in maintaining a
desert screen around the Suez Canal. Oil later became
an additional and complicating interest. The increasing American investment in Middle East oil does not
mean identity of interest between the United States
and Britain. In one aspect America is the partner and
supporter of Britain. In another, America is a com-
petitor tending to supplant Britain.

The international politics of oil have been already
developed; the effect of oil on the domestic politics of
the Arab states has yet to gather momentum. Up to the
present, royalties paid on oil have in the main been
perquisites of the hereditary Arab rulers. As nationalist
feeling develops, there will be pressure for more and
more desk jobs and technical positions for Arabs in the
refineries and oil fields, in addition to coolie employment. It is impossible, however, to educate enough
Arabs for these jobs without having some of them turn
their attention to politics. The only possible course
that internal politics can take is pressure on the hereditary princes to make them surrender their private roy-
alty incomes to the state. The Union of India is already

setting precedents for this kind of development in the Indian princely states which it has taken over.

Turkey is a country that once had Soviet backing against Europe, now has American backing against Russia, and will inevitably develop the skill to play America against Russia. The eventual significance of Turkey as a country that can or cannot be used for the containment of Russia will become clearer only when a more stable relationship between the Balkans and Greece can be worked out. Here, as almost everywhere in Asia, it is impossible to have a clear-cut policy for one country alone. In the meantime, American support for Turkey has produced a crisis within Turkey. The arms which Turkey receives under the Truman Doctrine require Turkey itself to spend more than half of its budget to keep up an army large enough to use the arms. In Turkey, as in Greece, the Truman Doctrine creates as big a problem as the one it hopes to solve.

Israel is the most dynamic country in Asia. Because of the refugees and exiles who have gathered there, it probably has a higher concentration of the most modern skills and techniques in proportion to population than any other country in the world, including the United States. No other country so nearly approaches the impossible standard of a population consisting entirely of the elite. Other countries in the Near and Far East are struggling with the problem of evolving a modern urban civilization out of their ancient agri-

cultural and pastoral cultures. Israel has had the problem of converting city dwellers into farmers, and has
been able to solve the problem brilliantly by the massive use of technicians and scientists.

Israel exemplifies the best culture of Europe at a
very high level of evolution, but it is not revolutionary. Israel's presence in Asia, however, is revolutionary. Nowhere else in Asia is the scientifically
skilled and culturally mature European in direct contact with the ragged, depressed, and oppressed peoples
of the East as a farmer and artisan, a worker with his
hands. The nearest equivalent is where Russians and
Asians meet; but the average attainments of the Russian in Asia are not as high as those of the average
Israeli. And nowhere, outside of Russia, is it possible
for working Europeans to ask Asian workers to join
their labor unions with equal rights, as has happened in
Haifa, where the Israelis have extended their labor
rights to Arabs.

It is absolutely impossible to prevent this kind of
contact from being revolutionary in its effects. As an
obvious example, the poor Arab who once could not
think of social promotion except in the form of becoming a richer Arab, but still not a modern man, now
cannot escape the realization that in many ways it is
better to be a modern man than a rich Arab. He
realized this, of course, in a fairy-tale way when he
admired the marvelous possessions of the British effendi whom he occasionally saw. But there is no practical pathway to be traveled from ragged Arab to
British effendi. Living side by side with the Israeli,

however, he sees both the desirable and the practicable. Then comes the revolutionary jump: it is not the Israeli who prevents him from living as a modern man, but the Arab ruler.

A quick roll call of the countries which were once the strongholds of imperialism brings out problems of policy that tend to be overlooked when the policy makers concentrate on one country at a time. One thing that becomes evident is that American and European interests in these areas are not identical. Sometimes there are conflicts between them. The rapid increase of American oil interests is accompanied by a demand for control of strategic air bases and air routes. In naval power there is a tendency for the Mediterranean, which was once almost a British lake, to become more and more an American lake. In the Mediterranean and Near East America is engaged partly in supporting British policy and partly in superseding British interests. Where the British no longer have the strength to hold on and must hand over to America, it is natural for them to try to make the transfer in such a way that America will have to carry on as much of the old British policy as possible, and protect British investments and interests as far as possible, instead of simply superseding them and putting a squeeze on British investments and trade. The other thing that stands out is that there can in fact be no such thing as a successful policy tailored for only one colonial country. A successful policy for any one country must be carefully dovetailed into policies for other countries, which means that the old claim of European empires to exclusive sovereignty over their colonial possessions has become an obstacle that prevents any of them from carrying out successful policies. And since colonial instability makes these countries unstable in Europe, where America is trying to prop them up with the Marshall Plan and range them in line through the Western Union and the North Atlantic Pact, policy in Asia has become for America something that must be studied as part of the same complex as policy in Europe.

CHAPTER X

THE ESSENTIALS OF AN AMERICAN POLICY IN ASIA

THE title of this chapter is exactly the same as the title of the last chapter of *Solution in Asia*, which was published in 1945, before the surrender of Japan, and forecast the policy problems that would arise at the end of the war. The contents of the two chapters are not identical, but I have chosen the same title again in order to emphasize one of the elementary rules of policy making: problems of policy are continuous, and stem out of each other at successive stages, in such a way that even when the same kind of policy is followed or proposed, it must adapt itself in details to the changing situations which it is intended to manage.

It was obvious from the beginning, for instance, that independence was the key issue in Korea; but when Korea was divided at the 38th parallel for military occupation purposes, American policy made the fundamental error of allowing American–Russian prestige quarrels in a divided Korea to take precedence over the issue of a united Korea. By recognizing that this was a blind alley, giving up the prestige quarrel, and being the first to withdraw their troops, the Russians have reopened the main issue of Korean unity. By so doing they have won an advantage, making the American occupation forces in South Korea the foreign symbol of a divided country.

Another elementary rule is that when a mistake in policy has been made and it becomes necessary to go back to the point where things began to go wrong, it is almost always impossible to start over again in an attempt to do things the same way, only better. It is usually necessary to branch off at an angle. A sound policy must do more than acknowledge that there are such things as growth and change. It must operate within the laws of growth and change.

As an example, American policy at the end of the war sought to slow down the rate of change in Asia and to give priority to the political stabilization and economic recovery of Europe. Since then, however, in spite of American policy, the rate of change in Asia has been greater than the rate of recovery in Europe. We should therefore recognize the necessity of adapting our policy to the changing realities; and we can only do so by relaxing our pressure on Asia to subordinate its interests to our interests and those of Europe, and by increasing our pressure on Europe to join us in a policy of negotiating compromises on terms acceptable to Asia.

A sound policy springs from two roots: the character of the problem to which the policy is to be applied, and the character of the country which wants to solve the problem, or to maneuver it into a situation in which it can be managed. The most perplexing situations in American foreign policy have developed from our mistake in ignoring the fact that policy has these two roots. The Truman Doctrine, the consequences of which are now baffling us, is defective as a workable American policy because it fails to meet the true character of the problem in assuming that Greece and Turkey are the kind of country today to which British balance-of-power politics were applied in the nineteenth century. It also ignores the character of America today in the equally mistaken assumption that America has the same kind of power that Britain had in the nineteenth century. The Truman Doctrine originated more in out-of-date British thinking than in up-to-date American thinking. It is the child of the Fulton, Missouri, speech at which President Truman sat on the platform while Winston Churchill rang down the Iron Curtain.

A sound policy must be easily and quickly adaptable to both threats of war and opportunities of peace. In drafting such a policy, the biggest obstacle in the path of the President and the State Department is the widespread conviction that it is craven appeasement even to discuss the adjustments and compromises that are necessary to achieve peace, in a situation in which America cannot force Russia to retreat all along the line any more than Russia can force America to retreat all along the line.

All American policy must give full weight to the importance of power politics, because never before in history have the components and units of power been so massive and so easy to mobilize and bring into play. Since the end of the war, however, one of the defects of our policy has been obsession with what power can do — our own and that of Russia — to the point of neglecting the limits of power. It is as dangerous to maneuver in power politics without a precise knowledge of the limitations of the power that is being used as it is to load a gun with a bullet that is too large for the bore. The attempt to bring the course of change in China under American management failed because there were fundamental mistakes in measuring the pressure for change in China, and hence it was not realized that the American power that was being applied was not right for the job either in kind or in quantity.

Sound power politics must take the measure of the possibilities of peace as well as war. Since the Truman-Churchill Doctrine there has been so strong an emphasis on the danger of another war and the necessity for preparedness that American policy has to a definite and dangerous extent hampered its own maneuverability if it should turn out, in the next few years, that peace is preferable to war because no "big" war can be fought under conditions that suit the kind and amount of strength that America has. It is disastrous to be caught in a war situation with only a peace policy and peace preparations. It can also be extremely dangerous to be caught with a policy overweighted toward war and war preparations in a situation in which peace offers the best opportunities for strengthening and advancing American interests.

Politics has its own law of probabilities. The trend

of the world in any period of history always creates conditions under which some things are rather likely to happen while other things are rather unlikely to happen. The strength of this trend always varies from one part of the world to another.

The first step toward sound policy is to forecast this contemporary trend as accurately as possible, and to check on its variations in different parts of the world. Frequently it is impossible to prevent a development that has too high a momentum of probability. A trend that cannot be absolutely stopped can, however, very often be deflected; a development that cannot be controlled can usually be influenced. Correspondingly, a development that has not quite enough momentum of probability of its own can often be helped along by the right kind of policy.

The second step toward sound policy is therefore to forecast our own resources in terms of trends that can be stopped, controlled, influenced, or promoted.

The third step is to forecast our ability to combine our own policy resources with those of other countries, and to forecast what we shall have to offer and what we shall have to accept in order to get as much as possible of what we ourselves want.

The practice of policy is the combination of these changeable elements with enough flexibility to take advantage of opportunities that turn out to be bigger than we had foreseen, and to evade or cushion the shock of setbacks for which we had not made enough allowance in advance.

In applying these maxims to Asia we must start from

the probability that in the next few years the area in Asia that we are able to control, either by ourselves or in association with other countries, will shrink, while the area that is out of control will expand. It is also conservative and realistic to forecast that Russia's power to control Asia will not expand nearly as fast as the power of America and Europe to control Asia diminishes. In the gap there will arise a group of "third countries," which cannot be counted into our line-up but will be able to deal with us and get along with us. They will also be able to deal with Russia and get along with Russia, without becoming puppets controlled outright by Russia.

The emergence of these third countries is an altogether healthy phenomenon. There is a possibility that a successful third-country development in China, the Union of India, Pakistan, and perhaps later Japan and Indonesia, might encourage a trend toward third-country development in Europe. Sweden, Norway, and Denmark already have a strong third-country trend. Yugoslavia might become such a country; so might Austria. Eventually France and Italy might become third countries as part of a general trend, although they cannot be made into such countries by the third-force parties which they have at present.

We must next consider what kind of country is the America which so urgently needs to revise its policies in Asia. America is the strongest private-enterprise country in the world, and there are all kinds of jobs, all over the world, that can be done better by American private enterprise than by any other agency.

American prosperity will need the stimulus of these jobs abroad. They can be successfully undertaken in any kind of country, including Communist-controlled countries, in the manner of the pioneering jobs that Ford Motors and General Electric did in Russia in the period between wars.

American private enterprise, however, stands increasingly isolated in the world. Its strongest ally, British private enterprise, is being taken over stage by stage by socialized enterprise. The trend is so strong that even if a Tory Government were voted into power in the General Election due in 1950, it would not be able to reverse much of the legislation carried through by the Labour Government. In America itself, the environment of private enterprise is changing. Private enterprise needs wider opportunities abroad partly because the field is narrowing in America. Government regulation is increasing, and the trend is toward more regulation, not less. In addition, there is actual competition between public enterprise and private enterprise, particularly in undertakings like TVA which actually create new sources of wealth.

In this changing America organized labor in the next four years will for the first time seriously challenge organized private enterprise in exerting an influence on foreign policy. Changes in Asia will speed up the development of labor's interest in foreign relations. On the one hand, employment in America can be increased if America takes a hand in the industrialization of China, and if this means coming to terms with a Communist-dominated China, labor will not allow an American "sulky boycott" of China like Bevin's boycott of Israel. On the other hand, now that India and Pakistan have risen above colonial status, what remains of the colonial system in Asia, especially in Malaya and Indonesia, looks more and more like a vast collection of big business bonanzas in mines and plantations. It will not be long before American labor begins to ask whether American policy in these countries is primarily protecting profits at the expense of human rights, and to demand a policy that is beneficial to American employment as well as to American employers.

The politics of oil is especially vulnerable to attack by the labor interest in foreign policy. Investment in oil outside of America contributes practically nothing to full employment in America. Most of the oil in Asia, especially in the Arab states and the Near East, is found in countries where there is no political check on the feudal power of the hereditary rulers, and no protection for labor. The rulers, however, can maintain "peace and order" in the interests of the American investors who pay them royalties on their oil. There is consequently a very heavy pressure on the investors to support reactionary policies. In the past this has not exposed them to general criticism in America; but the criticism is bound to increase. We must not forget that there is also oil in countries like China, Indonesia, and Burma, where politics are already modern, as compared with the feudal politics of the Near East. Every improved oil agreement negotiated in these more advanced countries will hasten the maturing of domestic and international issues in the oil politics of the Near East.

The United States is the most powerful country in the world, but it is already clear that even American power cannot reach into all parts of the world with equal effect at all times. The limits of American power and the degree to which Asia is passing out of control mean that American policy must team up with the policies of some countries and come to an understanding with other countries that is far short of hostility in one direction, but far short of alliance in the other.

These requirements provide a scale of priority. First, America must work in virtual alliance with Britain and, if possible, France. This close association is already foreshadowed in the proposed North Atlantic Pact, the nucleus of which is the Western Union of Britain, France, Belgium, Holland, and Luxembourg. This alliance or near alliance has its own limitations, one of which is that the European countries cannot be treated as satellites, completely obedient to American orders. They can bring their own pressures to bear on America. A second limitation is that Britain no longer completely controls either the British Empire or the British Commonwealth. Pakistan and the Union of India, especially the Union of India, now hold to a degree that must be respected the power to make the British Commonwealth work smoothly, if they go along with it willingly, or badly, if they do not approve of its policies.

A third limitation on the effectiveness of America's

European allies is the colonial problem. This problem is likely to get more out of control rather than more under control, and not too much time is left before it begins to spread from Asia to Africa. Even complete agreement between America, Britain, France, and Holland cannot now make it possible to reduce Indonesia, Malaya, and Indo-China to unresisting obedience. On the other hand it is not to the interest of the colonial countries to wreck the economy of Europe. All of them have in fact suggested economic compromise with Europe even while insisting on political freedom. They are on the winning end of this argument. Some immediate compromise will have to be found, and America will have to be a party to it, because the colonial countries still trust America, in spite of many disillusionments, more than they do their European rulers.

Next in order of priority come relations with the "third countries," the most important of which are China, the Union of India, Pakistan, and probably, within a few years, Japan. These countries have two powerful bargaining points in dealing with America. They can make it either much more easy or much more difficult to settle the colonial problem. And, by refusing to act as an American front line against Russia, they can make us bid for the terms on which they will not act as a front line for Russia against the interests in Asia of America and Europe.

The Mongolian People's Republic (Outer Mongolia) belongs in a special category on the fringe of the third-country classification. It would be to the

American interest to bring Mongolia nearer to third-country status. Instead we have made the mistake of voting against Mongolia as a member of the United Nations, alleging that there is doubt about whether it is in fact independent. The point is that Mongolia was for years sandwiched between the Soviet Union and a non-Communist China. In this period the Mongols were more afraid of China than of Russia. On the Russian side there was always the danger of control, but on the Chinese side there was the danger of complete obliteration through Chinese colonization.

Now Mongolia is between a Communist-ruled Russia and a Communist-controlled China. In this situation it would be an advantage to American policy to be able to emphasize that there is a country, occupying 600,000 square miles of territory in the frontier zone between China and Russia, inhabited by people who are neither Chinese nor Russians. It is impossible to make use of this advantage unless the separation of Outer Mongolia is emphasized by membership in the United Nations and there are direct relations and an exchange of diplomatic representatives between America and Mongolia. It is true that Mongolia as a member of the United Nations would mean another vote for Russia; but would this be a greater disadvantage than our present complete lack of access to this key country between China and Russia? American recognition of Mongolia would have been much more advantageous if it had been effected before the great changes in China; but it is not too late now.

Third in order of priority come relations with Russia, which, though much less powerful than America, is the only country in the world powerful enough to take an individual stand against America and to range a group of allies, satellites, and sympathetic countries against the group of countries that look to America for backing. If the first two priorities in American foreign policy can be dealt with satisfactorily, it will be possible to substitute a cold truce for the present cold war with Russia. If not, the cold war will continue under conditions that will probably swing slowly in favor of Russia, because our allies in Europe are willing to be supported and subsidized to prevent the infiltration of Communism, but are much less willing to be sacrificed if America, feeling that the cold war against Russia is not going well, should want to switch to a hot war.

These three steps of priority mean that American policy, to be successful, must operate through the United Nations as much as possible and strengthen the United Nations as much as possible. A two-world system of American allies and satellites, ranged against Russian allies and satellites, is not enough in America's favor and may be too much in Russia's favor. Only by working through the United Nations can the third countries, which are already critically important in Asia and may become important in Europe, be brought closer to the American side than to the Russian side.

The State Department is extremely sensitive to the suggestion that America has weakened or by-passed the United Nations. The sensitivity is understandable, because the State Department has to make the official statements that are intended to cover up not only its own mistakes but those of the President and the Congress — and the least defensible mistakes that it is forced to try to defend are those of the 80th Congress. Yet the truth, which no official alibis can hide permanently, is that the most successful American policies have been those that were carried out through the United Nations; the most disastrous have been those that by-passed the United Nations.

UNRRA, a United Nations operation for which America supplied most of the money, was an outstanding success — except in China, where the United Nations had no authority or influence. In Eastern Europe, White Russia, and the Ukraine, what remains of friendly feeling for America is due primarily to the operations of UNRRA, in which American selfish interests were soft-pedaled while American goods were loud-pedaled.

Even more outstanding was the success of the pressure exercised through the United Nations which resulted in the withdrawal of the Russians from Iran in 1947. Washington has not yet learned the lesson of this retreat. It has now become an obsession with Washington that the Russians, somewhere in the world, must back off in the face of direct American pressure. Only after they have made a token retreat of some kind acknowledging that America, without the United Nations, is stronger than Russia will Washington consent to talk about deals and agreements. This kind of American pressure, outside of the United Nations, has been a flat failure. We should take up issues between ourselves and Russia in the form that emphasizes political strength in the United Nations, not in the form that emphasizes military strength outside the United Nations.

On the other hand the Truman Doctrine on Greece and Turkey, which would be less embarrassing and more accurately described if it were known as the Churchill Doctrine, by-passed the United Nations. It has led to a situation in which America cannot acknowledge failure for fear of seeming to admit defeat by Russia, while Russia cannot seek a compromise for fear of seeming to yield to America. The Marshall Plan also by-passed the United Nations. If, like UNRRA, it had been routed through the United Nations it would have been impossible for Russia to keep Poland and Czechoslovakia from participation, and difficult for Russia itself to stay out. The Marshall Plan has been a partial success, but it cannot be more than that because even the Europeans who are helped by it are convinced that it was not intended to unify the world economically, but to divide it permanently into American-controlled and Russian-controlled areas.

The American effort to slow down the rate of change in China and make it manageable also by-passed the United Nations. The idea of a manageable rate of change was in itself admirable. It might have succeeded if carried out through the United Nations, in such a manner as to assure the Chinese that they were not being put on the firing line of an American policy against Russia, and would not later be transferred into the firing line of a Russian policy against America. It could not succeed as a purely American policy. Its failure left America with an exposed flank in Asia, and with a damaged prestige that could not be spread over the members of the United Nations.

We shall get nowhere if, every time one of the two great powers makes a concession, it looks like a direct increase of power for the other. Statesmanlike adjustments can best be made through the United Nations, in forms that strengthen its authority. At present the United Nations is in danger of becoming a parade ground on which one regiment of countries lines up with a yes-vote for Russia and another with a yes-vote for America. We should take the lead over Russia in changing the United Nations into an organization into which increasing strength can be built. To do so it is necessary to change the practice of by-passing it every time it is hoped an advantage can be gained for America, and appealing to it only when a deadlock is expected. It should be through the United Nations, not outside of it, that we assure the peoples to whom our policies are applied that they are being built into a world order in which all sacrifices are shared, and all benefits are pooled.

If we cannot control Asia, we must get Asia to participate in our policies. Asia will not participate if it is convinced that it is being given a low priority in order to insure the recovery of Europe first; nor will it participate if it suspects that it is being made the victim of the hostility of one of the two giant powers of the world to the social, economic, and political system of the other giant power. If it comes to that kind of game, there are too many countries in Asia that can play off Russia and America against each other more successfully than either America or Russia can use them as pawns.

Recognizing the limitations that force us to admit that we no longer have control and must work through influence and the building up of mutual interests, we should begin our revision of policy at the European end. We should assure the European countries that are getting Marshall Plan aid and also have colonies that we do not approve of their using any of these funds for military purposes in Asia. Without making a unilateral decision, we should put forward the following policy to be discussed on a footing of equality with both Marshall Plan countries and their colonies:

1. Set aside, from present Marshall Plan grants, a fund proportionate to the importance of the colonies in the economic recovery of Europe.

2. Use this fund not as a Marshall Plan operation but as a new United Nations operation, a program of economic co-operation between the colonial countries and Europe aimed jointly at European economic recovery and colonial industrialization.

3. Set a premium on rapid emancipation by increasing the allocations to be shared between countries that have become fully independent and their former rulers.

4. Avoid the trap of demanding "peace and order"

as the price of aid to liberated colonies — a policy which only results in strong-man government on the surface and discontent under the surface. Peace and order should be the result achieved by sound policies, not the hold-up price asked for economic handouts.

Concurrently, there should be a declaration of American policy to cover such cases as Malaya, where an immediate grant of full independence would probably lead to increased bloodshed instead of peace. This declaration should state that in the American view a definite date should be set for full independence; the number of years to run before independence is achieved should be set by the United Nations, not by the ruling power, and it should be set after consultation with the people or peoples of each colony on a footing of equality, as well as with the ruler.

The Arab states and Iran are protectorates or spheres of influence rather than colonies. The chief issues are oil and strategic security. American policy could take a commanding lead by proposing a special kind of "oil trusteeship" under the authority of the United Nations. The principle should be that these countries should not suffer damage to their own long-term interests by having their oil exported to industrialized countries, while they receive only royalties.

All countries should be free to compete in operating oil concessions under general regulation by a United Nations Oil Authority. Competition should be open to both state enterprise and private enterprise. The country providing the oil should receive royalties which are funded to benefit the whole country and its people, not merely the privy purse of the hereditary ruler.

If oil politics are properly handled, the security issue will in large measure be settled automatically. The strengthening of the countries in between the Soviet Union and American and British interests will enable them to hold the rival great powers apart.

If policy for colonial Asia and the Near East is well drafted, it will make much simpler the formulation of policy toward such countries as Pakistan, the Union of India, Burma, Siam, and China. In all these countries American policy should avoid attaching itself to persons who thereby become identified as "agents" of American interests. In all these countries the American policy should respond to, and be aimed at, the policies of the countries themselves. The American interest in these countries is to cultivate the maximum field of legitimate operation for American private enterprise in trade, in contracting and engineering, and in supplying and installing machinery.

The countries of Asia have an interest of their own in encouraging this kind of American activity, which will offset whatever relations they have with Russia. America can supply what they need; Russia can supply very little. We must, however, accept the limitation that practically nowhere in Asia can we succeed for very long in demanding bad political relations with Russia as the price of good economic relations with America. Our bluff would be called too soon, and we had therefore better not even attempt the policy.

We shall also have to learn to do without political

controls or guarantees to safeguard the financial security of our investments. "Risk capital," the Chinese and Indians and others will say, "is entitled to the profits of risk capital. It is not entitled to the rewards of risk capital plus political guarantees which eliminate risk. Trade with us, take your profits, and come back for more, or — don't trade." Both China and India would like to trade with us and make more rapid progress; but they will be stable enough to survive, and to stand us off, if we do not give them fair commercial terms.

In expanding the legitimate activity of American private enterprise it is essential to recognize and encourage the aspirations of free private enterprise in the countries with which we deal. In all countries that are weak in their economic development there is a tendency for some businessmen to lean on stronger foreign enterprise. Throughout the Far East such men are known as compradores. They take a commission, as agents and brokers, on the deals they put through for foreign enterprise, and because of this relationship they tend to support any privileges or unequal economic advantages that may be enjoyed by foreign enterprise. They are disliked and politically distrusted in their own countries because they are dependent, not independent.

Free and nationalistic enterprise competes against these compradores. In the long run it is to the American interest that the compradore should be replaced by the independent businessman, because in no country in Asia can private enterprise be strong enough to

support and influence a government that is really independent unless it is itself genuinely independent.
In China and the Philippines especially there is deep
distrust of the businessman whose influence on the
government is suspected of serving as a channel for
the pressure of foreign interests.

American policy can help to build up the independent businessman in Asia by consenting promptly
to the revision of treaties such as those signed with
China and the Philippines after the war. These treaties
were drawn up in the name of a spurious "equality,"
giving Chinese and Filipino businessmen the "legal"
right to engage in some of the same activities in America that are permitted American businessmen in China
and the Philippines. In the case of the Philippines,
Americans were granted rights which Philippine
citizens do not have in the United States. Such treaties
follow the letter but evade the spirit of the American
principle of encouraging freedom of trade all over the
world — especially when America continues to maintain its own tariff protection. The treaties must be
revised because no country in Asia can make itself
economically strong and sound unless it can pass laws
favoring the development of its own independent
industries. America is entitled to equality in competition with other countries outside of Asia for investment and trade in Asia, but not to advantages, in any
country, over the businessmen of that country.

An American policy of cordiality toward a third-
country type of political and economic independence
will make possible a sound Japan policy. In a very few

years Japan can become one of the most important
third countries — but only if it is as free to make agreements with China, Russia, and India as with America.
The limiting factor for United States policy is the fact
that the Japanese are politically so experienced, and
economically so well organized and adaptable, that
they are already playing us against Russia more successfully than we can play them against Russia. This
situation is one that we cannot control. It is therefore
to our interest to negotiate a peace treaty with Japan
as soon as possible; to negotiate it as an internationally
agreed treaty and not as an American-dictated treaty;
and to end our occupation. Abandoning our attempt
to use Japan as the exclusive instrument of our policy
— because we cannot get away with it — we must
thereafter look to strengthening the United Nations
for the checks and balances we shall need in the adjustment of our relations with Russia.

There remains the question of our military position
in the North Pacific. We must get rid of the dangerous
illusions that Japan and South Korea, which politically
will become steadily more resentful of our presence
and control, can be of any lasting value to our military security. We must protect our own territory, and
we have the means to do so. We now control such a
deep screen of islands that we cannot be attacked
across the broad part of the Pacific either from Japan
or from bases in China. In addition we have Alaska,
which is our true bastion for all forms of defense, including offensive defense by the use of long-range
planes and projectiles. We do not need beachheads

from which to assault continental Asia, because Asia, strategically, is an area in which our ground strength would certainly be dissipated and could not possibly be concentrated.

Hitherto we have followed an emergency policy of trying to contain and oppose Russia with our own strength, while trying to build up support behind a front line that we hold virtually alone. Now we can reverse the approach. The colonial, colonial-European, and third-country policies that I have outlined would enable us to take up the adjustment of our relations with Russia backed by the good will of countries independent of us but benefiting by association with us, and therefore having a vested interest in remaining free of control by Russia.

The fundamental adjustment will then require the Russians to concede that capitalism is not withering or collapsing, while we shall have to concede that Communism cannot be extirpated by war. On our side, we shall have given a fresh impetus to both capitalism and political democracy. We shall have a strong competitive advantage in being able to help more people get what they want than the Russians can. We shall have turned the disadvantage of an Asia that we are not strong enough to control into the advantage of an Asia strong enough to refuse to be controlled by Russia. And by dovetailing policy in Asia with policy in Europe, instead of seesawing back and forth between the two, we shall have made possible the consolidation of third-country buffers in Europe as well as in Asia.

Throughout Asia today there prevails an atmosphere of hope, not of despair. There is not a single country in Asia in which people feel that we are entering on an age of chaos. What they see opening out before them is a limitless horizon of hope — the hope of peaceful constructive activity in free countries and peaceful co-operation among free peoples. There will be disillusionments along the way as these hopes unfold. They should not come from America, or as the result of American policy. A great part of Asia's hopes, however, will be fulfilled, and should be fulfilled with American co-operation. We have everything to gain by being on the side of hope.

Index

INDEX

Index